Soup for All Occasions

RECIPES FOR ENJOYING LIFE

A simple bowl of soup
can make any
occasion special

NEW COVENT GARDEN FOOD Co

Soup for All Occasions

RECIPES FOR ENJOYING LIFE

B▦XTREE

We, New Covent Garden Food Company, would like to say a huge thank you to everyone who kindly gave us their recipes and were happy for us to share them with you all in this, our fourth recipe book. There are too many to list here but they're mentioned on the recipes themselves.

We would, however, like to give a special thank you to our chief taster, Sian Grist, our copy creator, Richard Cooke, and Mike Edwards, who drew all the lovely pictures.

First published 2009 by Boxtree, an imprint of Pan Macmillan Ltd
Pan Macmillan, 20 New Wharf Road, London N1 9RR
Basingstoke and Oxford
Associated companies throughout the world
www.panmacmillan.com

ISBN 978 0 75222 679 8

1 3 5 7 9 8 6 4 2

A CIP catalogue record for this book is available from the British Library.

Printed and bound in Italy by Printer Trento S.r.l.

Visit www.panmacmillan.com to read more about all our books and to buy them. You will also find features, author interviews and news of any author events, and you can sign up for e-newsletters so that you're always first to hear about our new releases.

Contents

Introduction

An unusual passion for soup

We think soup is the most wonderful thing to eat. This is hardly surprising as soups are our passion and have been for quite a while. Whether they are fresh in a carton or in the form of a recipe for you to try at home, new fresh ideas keep coming. The flow of new recipes never seems to dry up, as they are thought up by everyone from our chefs in the kitchen to our colleagues in the accounts office, as well as all our families and friends.

So it is time for a new recipe book – our fourth – packed with novel ideas for making and using that most versatile of meals: lovely soup. This collection shows just how many times soup provides just the right meal. That's why we've called this book *Soup for All Occasions.*

Whether you're pondering how to impress guests at a dinner party or scratching your head over how to feed a family gathering in the garden, there is a soup here that will fit the occasion.

Not only is soup highly versatile, it's usually easy to make without a great deal of mess, invariably healthy and nutritious and often a great way of using up leftovers. When you see how easily soup fits into whatever you're doing, you'll know why we love it so much.

Soup for All Occasions

There are all sorts of recipes here: some are classics with a new twist or an unusual extra ingredient; some are completely fresh ideas from our experimenting chefs. There are soups for all seasons and any time of day – from a summer garden party to a winter lunch for hungry walkers. As an extra treat, you'll find ideas that stretch the definition of soup a bit: stews and smoothies – even breakfasts. Don't be put off; just try them out. It'll be fun.

For simple and quick-to-make recipes, the 'Soups for Everyday' chapter offers you tasty and nutritious ideas for informal meals with family and friends – or just for you.

Sometimes you will want to make more of an impression on your friends. `Soups for Entertaining´ is a collection of the spectacular, the innovative and the unusual. Only you will know how easy most of them are to make.

When you have a theme to your entertaining, turn to `Soups for Calendar Occasions´. Here you'll find ideas for lovers on Valentine's Day, families on bonfire night, kids at Halloween and unusual recipes for a festive Christmas.

The transportability of soup is one of its greatest virtues. With `Soups for Out & About´ all you need is a flask and a mug and you have just the thing for a stiff walk across the hills, a posh picnic or the kids' lunchboxes.

Every now and then any chef needs to cheat a little, so we've put together a chapter which will give you some shortcuts that no-one will notice. `Occasions When We Need to Cheat´ will also show you how to use ready-made fresh soups from our range to create delicious meals for family and friends.

All the help you need

We're enthusiastic about soup and we have lots of people on our team who think about virtually nothing else. We've put all they know into these recipes, making sure they work well and are easy to follow. We've also given you loads of tips for serving, with ideas for garnishes and side dishes and some alternative ingredients that may be useful.

As you scan through the recipes on offer you will see how many different ways there are of using soup to nourish, satisfy and entertain. That's why we can confidently say that there is a soup for any occasion. And of course when you really have no time at all, you will always find a carton or two of our fresh soups on the shelf at your local store.

Soups for Everyday

Breakfasts   Lunches   Dinners

Soups for Everyday

When you want a tasty and nutritious meal, there are few things better than a bowl of soup. Soups are so versatile and adaptable that there's not much chance of you getting bored.

Some people only cook a soup when they are preparing a special dinner; some think it's a nutritious way of feeding a child who's under the weather. But who needs a particular reason for making soup? What about everyday?

Here are some new ideas for any time you feel like a soup.

To help you keep ringing the changes, our chefs have put on their thinking caps and come up with this collection of recipes. They are mostly simple and inexpensive ways of making an appealing and healthy meal for you and your family.

There are ideas here for hearty evening meals, light lunches and filling breakfasts – yes, breakfasts. If anyone tells you that soup is boring, surprise them with our alternative to a full English breakfast.

Sausage, Bacon & Tomato

Who loves a full English breakfast? We think it's the perfect start to the weekend, so we've been working out the best way to get the same excitement into a soup. This is also somewhat healthier than the traditional fry-up.

Topped with a fried egg, this is a tactile dish; children like fishing for the sausages and bacon so it's a very involving way to get all the family well fed and ready for a fun-packed Saturday together.

Cooking time: 50 minutes

Serves 4

12 rashers smoked streaky bacon
4 eggs
12 chipolata sausages
4 tomatoes, halved
2 x 400g tins chopped tomatoes
2 tablespoons olive oil
1 small onion, finely diced
pinch of dried oregano
pinch of sugar
1 tablespoon fresh basil, chopped

- Chop 4 rashers of bacon. Heat the oil in a saucepan, then fry the bacon and onion until softened.
- Add the tinned tomatoes, herbs and sugar, then simmer gently for 20 minutes.
- Meanwhile, preheat the grill on a medium setting, season the tomato halves and grill with the sausages and bacon.
- When the tinned tomatoes and herbs are cooked, fry the eggs in a frying pan.
- Pour the tomato soup into serving bowls, then garnish with three sausages, two rashers of bacon and top with a fried egg. Serve with crusty bread.

Bircher Muesli

Here is a breakfast packed with goodness. There's no cooking needed – all you have to do is soak the oats overnight – so there's no excuse for skipping breakfast.

It is named after the good Dr Bircher-Benner, who created it to improve the diet of the rich burghers of Zurich who flocked to his clinic in the 1890s. He based his ideas on the simple healthy lifestyle of the shepherds in the Swiss Alps and changed breakfasts for ever.

Serves 4

Preparation time: 10 minutes plus 1 hour soaking time

200g rolled oats
300ml apple juice
1 green apple
1 pear
100g natural yogurt
1 lemon, juice of
150g mixed berries

- Place the oats and apple juice in a bowl, stir, then leave to soak for at least 1 hour, or ideally overnight.
- When the soaking of the oats and apple juice has finished ... leaving the skins on, grate the apple and pear, then add to the oats with the lemon juice and yogurt and stir well.
- Serve topped with the mixed berries.

Kedgeree

This great British tradition is actually Indian in origin. We thought it well worth reviving the dish of a more relaxed age for a lazy Sunday morning brunch with family or guests as you linger over the morning papers.

This is the real thing: an eating indulgence with a gorgeous colour and a hint of spice. The very little extra effort in the kitchen is well worth it.

Cooking time: 50 minutes

Serves 4

2 eggs, hard boiled
550g undyed smoked haddock fillets
600ml water
1 medium onion, finely diced
2 teaspoons curry powder
2 lemons
1 tablespoon fresh coriander, finely chopped
2 tablespoons flat leaf parsley, finely chopped
1 bay leaf
75g butter
1 tablespoon olive oil
200g Basmati rice

- Juice 1 of the lemons, then cut the other into wedges and set aside.
- Place the haddock in a large sauté pan, add the water to cover the haddock, then bring to the boil. Cover and simmer for 5 minutes until just cooked.
- Drain off the cooking liquid and set to one side. Wrap the haddock in foil to keep warm.
- Melt 50g butter in the same pan you cooked the haddock in, fry the onion until soft, then add the curry powder and cook for 1 minute.
- Add the rice to the onion, stir well to coat it, then add the set-aside cooking liquid. Bring to a simmer, cover, then gently heat for 10–15 minutes.
- Meanwhile, skin and flake the haddock into large chunks, then peel the eggs and cut them into wedges.
- When the rice is cooked, gently stir in the haddock, coriander, half the parsley, juice of 1 lemon and the remaining butter, then fork through to combine.
- Sprinkle over the remaining parsley and serve with the lemon wedges.

Red Berry Smoothie

Rebecca Pope works hard selling our soups. After her morning run she wants a breakfast which will set her up for a busy day without undoing all the good from her pavement pounding. What with the running and the shower afterwards she doesn't have a lot of time, so all her breakfasts have to be quick and easy to make.

Her favourite is this healthy burst of freshness. All it takes is a quick whizz of the blender and in five minutes she is enjoying her tangy smoothie. Rebecca uses frozen berries, which work fantastically in smoothies, so all she has to do is grab a handful from the freezer.

Serves 2

Preparation time: 5 minutes

250g mixed berries, equal quantities of each (we use a mix of raspberries, blueberries and strawberries)
200g natural yogurt
100ml apple juice
crushed ice (optional)

- Place the berries, yogurt and apple juice in a blender, along with some crushed ice if you like a thick smoothie, then blend until smooth.
- Serve in tall glasses.
- Add a drizzle of honey if you like it a little sweeter.

Winter Fruit Compote with Granola

This warming dish is a festive favourite of Sue Farrow, the first voice you'll hear when you call us. As the fruit and spices simmer, the inviting aromas make sure that all her family gather round the kitchen table.

When she serves this on Christmas morning with yogurt and granola, the kids have to be prised away to open their presents. Better still, Sue knows that the family are filled with healthy goodness before they get distracted by sweets and crisps.

Serves 4

Cooking time: 30 minutes

100g dried apricots
100g dried dates
100g dried prunes
100g berries and cherries mix
4 cloves
1 cinnamon stick
400ml boiling water
500g Greek yogurt
8 tablespoons granola

- Place the apricots, dates, prunes, berries and cherries mix, cloves and cinnamon stick in a saucepan, then pour over the boiling water.
- Cover and simmer for 30 minutes.
- Allow to cool slightly before removing the cinnamon stick and cloves.
- Serve warm (or at room temperature) with a dollop of thick yogurt and sprinkled with granola.

Banana & Chocolate Frappucino

In the hot-house atmosphere of our creative kitchens, some strange things get discussed, not least the use of all sorts of leftovers. When the subject of what to do with cold coffee came up, one of our inventive chefs took up the challenge and created this gorgeous breakfast idea.

With its frothy texture and great mix of flavours, this will really charge the batteries so you can hit the ground running.

Serves 2

Cooking time: 5 minutes plus cooling

250ml cafetiere coffee
2–3 teaspoons hot chocolate powder
100g frozen vanilla yogurt
1 banana
250ml milk
crushed ice to serve

- Make a cafetiere of strong coffee and allow to go cold before using.
- Place the coffee, hot chocolate powder, yogurt, banana and milk in a blender and blend until smooth.
- Either add crushed ice to the blender and blend once again or pour over crushed ice to serve.

Simple Pea Soup

This good looking, fresh tasting green soup is a favourite of Chris Moxon, whose job is to make each recipe better than the last. Being a chef he can put together a simple dish like this with his eyes closed. However, because he's one of our chefs, he's always experimenting.

For example, you can work this through a sieve, add a little coconut milk *et voilà*: you have a creamy *velouté* with a deliciously different taste that would grace any dinner table.

Serves 4

Cooking time: 20 minutes

500g frozen peas
50g butter
1 small onion, finely diced
1 small leek, finely diced
1 celery stick, finely diced
750ml chicken stock

- Melt the butter in a saucepan, then gently sauté the onion, leek and celery for 10 minutes until soft and transparent.
- Add the stock and simmer for 5 minutes.
- Add the peas, bring back to the boil and simmer for a further 3–4 minutes until the peas are just tender.
- Blend until smooth, season to taste and serve.

Courgette, Feta & Mint

We know these make a fantastic salad combination. But with just a little extra effort the flavours come together to create a light and tasty soup.

With toasted pitta bread on the side and some extra feta and mint, you have an ideal lunch to share with the girls. We've not known anyone who doesn't enjoy this. Indeed, it's so light and tasty it would be a good idea to be ready with second helpings.

Serves 4

Cooking time: 30 minutes

4–6 (850g) courgettes, cut into large chunks
2 tablespoons olive oil
1 clove garlic, crushed
600ml vegetable stock
50ml double cream
75g feta cheese
1 tablespoon fresh mint, finely chopped

- Heat the oil in a saucepan, then cook the courgettes and garlic over a medium heat for 20 minutes until soft and lightly browned.
- Add the stock and simmer for 5 minutes.
- Add the mint and feta cheese, then stir over a low heat until the feta has almost melted.
- Blend until smooth.
- Reheat gently, adding the cream before serving.
- Garnish with extra feta and mint if desired.

Cauliflower & Chive

We never get bored with this, so it's a good job it's as healthy as it is tasty. Cauliflower on its own is highly nutritious, but some people find it a little bland. Fortunately it seems to bring out the taste of other ingredients, like the fresh chives in this recipe.

The hint of chives gives an extra tangy taste to the velvety smoothness of the cauliflower. Using Greek yogurt rather than cream adds another dimension without drowning the other flavours.

Serves 4

Cooking time: 35 minutes

1 medium cauliflower, outer leaves removed, cut into small florets
1 medium potato, diced
25g butter
1 tablespoon olive oil
1 medium onion, finely chopped
650ml vegetable stock
4 tablespoons Greek yogurt
1 tablespoon chives, chopped

- Melt the butter in a saucepan, then add the onion and potato. Cover and sweat gently for 10 minutes until soft.
- Add the cauliflower florets and the stock to the saucepan, bring to the boil, then cover and simmer for 15–20 minutes until the cauliflower is tender.
- Blend until velvety smooth, then reheat gently, stirring in the Greek yogurt and chives.
- Season to taste before serving.

Ham & Pearl Barley

Amy Telfer, one of our chefs, has been thinking up recipes since her student days. Her mum used to pack her off to uni with leftovers from Sunday lunch, convinced that Amy was close to starvation in term-time.

By inventing this substantial hearty soup she certainly didn't starve. Her creation will work with any combination of stock and cooked meat, so she had plenty of variety as well as a nourishing diet as she studied hard.

Serves 4
Cooking time: 1 hour 10 minutes

30g pearl barley
30g green lentils
30g red split lentils
200g tinned haricot beans, rinsed and drained
800ml ham or chicken stock
1 medium potato, peeled and diced
250g cooked ham
2 medium carrots, diced
1 medium onion, finely diced
2 tablespoons olive oil
1 tablespoon fresh parsley, chopped

- Heat the oil in a saucepan, then fry the onions for 10 minutes until translucent.
- Rinse the lentils and pearl barley, then add to the saucepan, along with the carrots and stock.
- Bring to the boil before covering and simmering for 30 minutes.
- Shred the ham into bite-sized pieces and add the ham, haricot beans and potato to the saucepan. Simmer for a further 30 minutes.
- Check that all the pulses are cooked, adding extra stock or water to adjust the consistency.
- Season to taste, stir in the parsley and then serve.

Carrot & Cumin

Our Carrot & Coriander soup is loved by many and cartons fly off the shelves, so you'd expect another carrot soup recipe from us. So here's a different way of using this lovely colourful vegetable. Carrots store well and if you keep some handy, you will always be ready to put a soup together at the drop of a hat.

This has a fresh and zingy taste. Using water instead of stock lets the sweetness of the carrots come through to mix with the spices and lemon juice.

Serves 4

Cooking time: 35 minutes

600g carrots, sliced
900ml boiling water
1 medium onion, finely diced
1 clove garlic, sliced
50g butter
1 tablespoon sweet paprika
1 tablespoon ground cumin
2 teaspoons lemon juice
100ml milk
1 tablespoon chives, chopped

- Melt the butter in a saucepan, then add the carrots, onion, garlic, paprika and cumin. Stir, then cover and cook on a gentle heat for 20 minutes, stirring occasionally.
- Add the boiling water, bring back to the boil, then cover and simmer for a further 10 minutes until the carrots are tender.
- Blend until completely smooth, then add the milk and lemon juice.
- Reheat gently, season to taste and serve topped with chopped chives.

Tomato & Mascarpone

It seems that our PR guru, Carmel Mulhall, can't get enough of our Tomato & Mascarpone soup in the shops. She, like many others, has been badgering us for the recipe so she can make it at home.

No more letters on this please; of course we won't give away a secret like that, even for Carmel. However, to reward her persistence we have developed this recipe so that she – and you – can make a similar version at home.

Serves 4

Cooking time: 50 minutes

1 x 400g tin chopped tomatoes
1 heaped tablespoon mascarpone cheese
1 medium onion, diced
half clove garlic, finely chopped
5 tablespoons tomato puree
1 tablespoon caster sugar
2 tablespoons olive oil
3 tablespoons fresh basil leaves, chopped
320g passata
400ml water
pinch fresh rosemary, finely chopped
pinch dried oregano

- Heat the oil in a saucepan, then add the onion and garlic. Cook for 10 minutes until soft and translucent.
- Stir in the oregano, rosemary and tomato puree, then cook for a further 5 minutes.
- Stir in the passata, chopped tomatoes, sugar and water before bringing to the boil. Cover and simmer for 20 minutes.
- Stir in the basil, then blend until smooth.
- Reheat gently, season to taste, then stir in the mascarpone cheese. Continue to heat through gently, then serve.

Creamy Chicken

According to some old wives' tales, chicken soup is the cure for all conditions – from snow blindness to unrequited love. There's no doubt that there are few things more comforting than a steaming bowl of chicken soup, particularly on a chilly winter's day.

So whether you are comforting a friend or loved one, or just picking yourself up on a grey and miserable day, simply wrap your hands round a mug of this creamy delight. All your cares will just melt away.

Cooking time: 45 minutes

Serves 4

140g cooked chicken breast, diced
25g butter
2 medium potatoes, diced
1 tablespoon olive oil
1 medium onion, diced
1 small clove garlic, crushed
2 tablespoons plain flour
750ml chicken stock
100ml milk
1 tablespoon white wine

- Gently sauté the butter, oil, onion and garlic in a saucepan for 5–10 minutes until the onion is soft.
- Add the potatoes and stock, bring to the boil, then cover and simmer for 25 minutes.
- Blend until smooth, then add the wine and cooked chicken.
- Mix the flour with a little water to form a paste and add to the pan. Whisk it in, then stir until simmering and thickened.
- Add the double cream and milk, then season to taste and serve.

Puy Lentil & Bacon

Puy lentils come only from Le Puy-en-Velay in France's Massif Central. They're noted for a unique peppery taste and for being high in protein but low in carbohydrates. Puy are our favourite lentils because they also hold their shape in cooking.

Because of that, this soup freezes well, so it's ideal for making in larger batches to give you a healthy and full flavoured soup ready for unexpected visitors.

Serves 4

Cooking time: 50 minutes

120g Puy lentils, rinsed
2 tablespoons olive oil
12 rashers smoked streaky bacon, chopped
1 medium onion, finely chopped
1 medium carrot, diced
1 clove garlic, crushed
1 x 400g tin chopped tomatoes
850ml chicken stock
5–6 sprigs fresh thyme
1 tablespoon fresh parsley, chopped
1 tablespoon tomato puree
1 bay leaf

- Heat the oil in a saucepan, then fry the bacon for a few minutes until lightly browned.
- Add the onion, carrot and garlic, then cook for 5–10 minutes until softened.
- Add the stock, lentils, tomatoes, bay leaf, tomato puree and thyme sprigs, bring to the boil, then cover and simmer for 40 minutes until the vegetables and lentils are tender.
- Remove the thyme sprigs and bay leaf. Stir in the parsley, season to taste, add a little water if necessary and then serve.

Roasted Sweet Potato

Joe Carne, one of our student chefs, is a keen gardener with a taste for visiting historic houses. He often compares their vegetable gardens unfavourably with his own well tended plot. However, he was impressed by Alnwick castle where he found new ideas for his vegetable patch.

Of course you don't have to grow your own sweet potatoes to enjoy his latest creation – the ones in your local supermarket will do just as well.

Cooking time: 35 minutes

Serves 4

3–4 (600g) sweet potatoes, peeled and diced
1 medium onion, peeled and cut into 8 wedges
2 tablespoons olive oil
1 teaspoon ground cumin
750ml vegetable stock
4 tablespoons natural yogurt

- Preheat the oven to 200°C/400°F/gas mark 6.
- Place the sweet potato and onion in a roasting tin, drizzle with the olive oil and sprinkle over the cumin. Season a little, then toss together to coat evenly.
- Roast for 25–30 minutes until the vegetables are tender and have taken on some colour.
- Blend the roasted vegetables with the hot stock until completely smooth.
- Reheat gently in a saucepan, season to taste and serve with a dollop of natural yogurt on top.

Moroccan Lamb & Chickpea

Nigel Parrott, who decides what we put on the shelves next, discovered this substantial family soup while living in Morocco. Everyone likes it, including his dog, Bramble. After a quick burst of preparation, he (Nigel, not the dog) puts the soup in the oven and they head off for a brisk walk.

Nigel adds the lentils when they get back. The exhausted dog sleeps peacefully, dreaming of bones to come, while the family gathers round to enjoy a delicious, filling meal.

Serves 4

Cooking time: 2 hours

1 (350g) lamb shank
1 medium onion, finely chopped
2 tablespoons olive oil
2 cloves garlic, crushed
2 celery sticks, chopped
3 plum tomatoes, chopped
80g tinned chickpeas
60g green lentils, rinsed
1 lemon, juice of
750ml chicken stock
half teaspoon ground cinnamon
good pinch saffron
half teaspoon ground ginger
half teaspoon turmeric
few grates nutmeg
small handful fresh coriander, chopped
1 tablespoon tomato puree

- Preheat the oven to 180°C/350°F/gas mark 4.
- Heat the oil in a large casserole dish, then brown the lamb shank.
- Add the onion, celery and garlic and fry for a further 10 minutes until golden and softened.
- Add the spices, stir for a few minutes, then add the tomatoes, lentils, tomato puree and stock.
- Cover and cook in the pre-heated oven for 1 hour and 15 minutes.
- Add the chickpeas and return to the oven for a further 30 minutes until the pulses are tender.
- The lamb should now be tender enough to pull off the bone. Shred a little then return to the casserole dish, adding the lemon juice and coriander.
- Season to taste, reheat gently on the hob and serve.

Minestra

This brilliant way of using leftovers is a favourite of Rachael Wilford, one of our soup creators. She has always loved baked beans and so she set to work to include them in a soup recipe. The result is this quick and tasty variation on minestrone.

The mixture of store cupboard tins and whatever fresh vegetables you have to hand is very easy to assemble and gives a great-tasting meal every time.

Serves 4

Cooking time: 35 minutes

30g macaroni
1 small potato, diced
1 medium carrot, sliced
1 stick celery, diced
1 small onion, diced
1 clove garlic, crushed
1 x 400g tin chopped tomatoes
600ml vegetable stock
1 tablespoon tomato puree
2 tablespoons olive oil
1 bay leaf
4-5 sprigs thyme
1 x 200g tin baked beans

To garnish ...
        fresh basil leaves, torn
        cheese, grated

- Heat the oil in a saucepan, add the onion and garlic, then sweat over a medium heat for a few minutes.
- Add the carrot, celery and potato, then sweat for 5 minutes.
- Add the tomatoes, tomato puree, stock, sprigs of thyme and bay leaf before bringing to the boil. Cover and simmer for 20 minutes until the vegetables are almost tender.
- Add the macaroni and baked beans, then simmer for a further 10 minutes until the pasta is just cooked.
- Season to taste before serving topped with grated cheese and torn basil leaves.

King Prawn & Chorizo

With fresh or frozen prawns readily available from the supermarket, all you need to add are a few store cupboard ingredients to produce these wonderful Spanish flavours at a moment's notice.

We find that chorizo makes a great staple ingredient. The air-dried sausage lasts for ages and adds a depth of flavour to many dishes. We like it so much you'll find it crops up elsewhere in this book.

Serves 4

Cooking time: 30 minutes

125g chorizo, diced
200g tinned haricot beans, drained and rinsed
16 cooked king prawns
1 tablespoon olive oil
1 medium onion, finely chopped
1 red pepper, de-seeded and finely chopped
generous pinch chilli flakes
1 tablespoon fresh thyme, chopped
2 cloves garlic, chopped
1 teaspoon smoked sweet paprika
800ml chicken stock
1 tablespoon tomato puree
1 tablespoon flat leaf parsley, chopped

- Heat the oil in a sauté pan or saucepan, then fry the onion and red pepper for 5 minutes until they begin to soften.
- Add the chorizo, chilli flakes, thyme and garlic and stir frequently. Once the fat starts to run from the chorizo, add the paprika and keep stirring. The vegetables should have softened and the chorizo should be lightly browned.
- Add the stock, tomato puree and haricot beans, then simmer for 10 minutes.
- Add the king prawns and cook for a further 3–5 minutes.
- Serve immediately sprinkled with chopped parsley.

Leek & Potato

Leek and potato is another of our best selling soups. There seems to be something very comforting about the taste of leeks on a cold day.

This soup is a real winter warmer. It's smooth and tasty, and a simple way to a nutritious meal. Adding the extra diced vegetables in the last few minutes gives a little bite and an interesting variation in texture.

Serves 4

Cooking time: 50 minutes

2 medium floury potatoes (such as Maris Piper), diced
3 small leeks, finely diced
2 new waxy potatoes (such as Estima), cut into small dice
600ml water
half small onion, diced
25g butter
50ml single cream
75ml milk

- Melt the butter in a saucepan, add the onion and two-thirds of the leeks, then sweat for 10 minutes until the onion starts to soften and go translucent.
- Stir in the floury potatoes and cook for a further 5 minutes.
- Add the water and bring to the boil. Cover and simmer for 10 minutes until the potatoes and leeks are soft.
- Blend the soup until smooth, then stir in the waxy potatoes and remaining leeks and cook gently for a further 10 minutes until the potatoes and leeks are soft, stirring frequently to prevent sticking.
- Stir in the single cream and milk before warming through.
- Season to taste using salt and ground white pepper, then serve.

Broccoli & Stilton

This is often thought of as a posh soup – a luxurious indulgence when you want to impress guests that takes ages of careful kitchen work. But this one is in our everyday collection of soups because it takes just 25 minutes of simple preparation.

We're sure you'll enjoy your everyday indulgence. But you could, of course, use it for posh occasions and not let on how simple it is.

Serves 4

Cooking time: 25 minutes

450g broccoli florets
1 small potato, diced
25g butter
1 tablespoon olive oil
1 small leek, diced
800ml vegetable stock
1 clove garlic, crushed
100g–150g Stilton cheese
100ml double cream

- Melt the butter in a saucepan, add the leek, garlic and potato, then cover and sweat gently for 10 minutes until soft.
- Add the broccoli florets and stock, bring back to the boil, then cover and cook for a further 6–8 minutes until the broccoli is just tender and has retained its colour.
- Stir in the Stilton cheese until it has almost melted, then add the cream.
- Blend until smooth, season to taste and serve.
- The amount of Stilton you use will depend on how mature it is and your personal taste. If you're a Stilton fan, crumble extra over the top.

Soups for Entertaining

Dinner Parties   Supper Parties   Desserts

Soups for Entertaining

A good soup recipe is a handy thing to have about you when you are entertaining. Whether you are crafting a dinner party to impress or having a few friends round after work, there's tons of inspiration for you here.

Our dinner party selection contains lots of new ideas and some unusual recipes that will make your guests sit up and take notice. Each is a brilliant way to start a meal, bring you a nod or two of approval and set the expectations for the rest of the evening.

For supper parties we got everyone to offer up their favourite recipes for less formal gatherings of friends or family. These are much more than your average soup. They just need crusty bread and a few trimmings to make a meal in themselves.

Then there are the sweet ones. Some would hesitate to call them soups, but when they are so colourful and tasty, who cares about strict definitions.

Asparagus, New Potato, Pea & Mint

The English asparagus season can be short, so lots of us like to fit in as many dishes as we can while the fresh green shoots are in abundance. At the height of the season it can be difficult to surprise dinner guests, particularly if they know you are an asparagus fan, but this delightful green creation will do it.

We top this refreshing light soup with asparagus spears and drizzle over lemon olive oil to bring out the spring flavours.

Serves 6

Cooking time: 25 minutes

4–6 (200g) new potatoes, peeled and diced
1 litre vegetable stock
250g peas, fresh or frozen
1 bunch asparagus, chopped into 2cm pieces
1 small pack (125g) fine asparagus spears (set aside the tips),
    stalks cut into 2cm pieces
1 small leek, diced
1 medium onion, diced
50g butter
1 tablespoon mint, chopped
drizzle of lemon olive oil

- Steam the asparagus tips for 2–3 minutes until *al-dente*, then refresh in cold water.
- Sweat the onion and leek in the butter and olive oil for 5 minutes, then add the potato. Cover and sweat without browning for a further 10 minutes, stirring occasionally to prevent sticking.
- Add the hot stock and chopped asparagus, then rapidly bring to the boil.
- Cover and simmer for 5–7 minutes, adding the mint and peas for the final 2 minutes.
- Blend in batches until very smooth. For a really silky finish, pass through a sieve.
- Reheat gently, season to taste, then serve with the asparagus spears on top and a drizzle of lemon olive oil.

Thai Prawn & Noodle Broth

Our Soup of the Month guru, Louise King, fell in love with Thai Cooking during her post-uni travels. She now claims to be the ultimate authority and enjoys impressing her friends with her new-found skills. This delicious light soup makes an excellent start to one of her banquets.

It's full of authentic exotic Eastern flavours and looks really stunning. Better still, it's much simpler to make than it looks, so Louise has time for the intricacies of the other courses.

Serves 6

Cooking time: 30 minutes

18 raw tiger prawns, shells on
2 sticks lemongrass, finely sliced
4 cloves garlic, peeled and finely sliced
2cm piece root ginger, peeled and finely sliced
1 large red chilli, de-seeded and finely sliced
10g (bunch) coriander, leaves and stalks separated
1 lime, juice of
1 litre fish stock
100g medium egg noodles
2 tablespoons soy sauce
1 tablespoon mint leaves, shredded
3 spring onions, finely sliced diagonally

- Remove the heads and shells from the prawns, leaving the tails on, then remove the veins.
- Place all the shells in a large pan, add the fish stock and 1 litre of water. Add the lemongrass, coriander stalks and half the garlic, then bring to the boil, skim and simmer for 20 minutes.
- Strain the stock into a clean pan, add the soy sauce, chilli and remaining garlic.
- Add the noodles and prawns and simmer for 3–4 minutes until the noodles and prawns are cooked.
- Add the lime juice and serve sprinkled with the spring onions, coriander and mint.

Tenderstem Broccoli & Dolcelatte®

Believe it or not, we know some people who claim not to like broccoli. Perhaps that's why some clever soup lover first came up with the popular broccoli and Stilton cheese combination. This posh version makes an impressive dinner party soup that everyone will like.

The sweet taste of the Dolcelatte goes well with the crunchy walnuts. We have heard that walnut has a calming effect so we serve with walnut bread to start a relaxing dinner.

Many thanks to our friends at Galbani for giving us their permission to include this recipe using Dolcelatte, their registered trademark.

Serves 6

Cooking time: 25 minutes

500g tenderstem broccoli, cut into 5cm pieces
1 small onion, finely chopped
1 small potato, diced
1 litre vegetable stock
2 cloves garlic
130g Dolcelatte cheese, diced
30g shelled walnuts, finely chopped
4 tablespoons double cream
2 tablespoons olive oil
1 tablespoon parsley, finely chopped

- Heat the oil in a pan and sweat the onions, garlic and potato for 10 minutes without browning.
- Add the broccoli and hot stock, then bring to a rapid boil. Cover and simmer for 6–8 minutes until the broccoli is just tender and has not lost its colour.
- Add the Dolcelatte and parsley, then stir until the cheese has melted.
- Blend before reheating and seasoning to taste.
- Serve with a drizzle of cream and a scattering of walnuts.

Dolcelatte® is a registered trademark of Galbani

Orange & Saffron Vichyssoise

Sometimes you have a group of dinner party guests who unnerve you a little: they've done it all, eaten it all. This unusual combination of flavours demands attention from the most jaded palette and will make your guests sit up and take notice.

It's a zingy, smooth soup that is delicious hot or chilled as a tasty *amuse bouche* – a pre-starter to tickle your taste buds – served in small bowls or coffee cups for a formal party. If you are serving canapés to guests standing up, it is equally good drunk from shot glasses.

Serves 6 (canapé size)

Cooking time: 35 minutes

3 (250g) young leeks, finely chopped
1 clove garlic, sliced
250g Jersey Royal new potatoes, peeled and diced
25g butter
750ml vegetable stock
5–6 strands saffron, infused in 50ml boiling water
4 oranges, juice of, plus zest of 1 orange
Caster sugar, to taste (caster sugar melts quicker than granulated)
Coriander, finely chopped, to garnish

- Sweat the leeks and garlic, without browning, for 5 minutes.
- Add the potato and sweat for a further 2–3 minutes.
- Add the stock and infused saffron, bring to the boil, then cover and simmer for 15 minutes.
- Blend, add the orange juice and pass through a sieve. Season to taste with salt, pepper and caster sugar (this will vary depending on the sweetness of your oranges).
- To serve chilled … refrigerate for several hours then serve in iced shot glasses, topped with the chopped coriander and a few shreds of orange zest.

Red Onion Soup with Goats' Cheese Toasts

'You can't start a dinner party with onion soup', said a concerned participant at one of our soup discussions. 'It's wonderful but hardly original.' Well here's a new way of turning the classic into an interesting start to a winter dinner party.

The wine adds sweetness and richness, while the goats' cheese toasts set off the red onions perfectly. If you're entertaining vegetarians, just use vegetable stock instead of beef. Even without the mouth-watering toasts, this is a filling soup, so keep the portions small if you want your guests to pay proper attention to the rest of the meal.

Serves 6

Cooking time: 1 hour

1.3kg red onions, finely sliced
4 tablespoons olive oil
25g butter
3 cloves garlic, crushed
1 tablespoon thyme, finely chopped
100ml marsala or port
1.2 litres beef stock
300g goats' cheese log, cut into thin slices
half pain parisien or french stick, cut diagonally into 1cm slices

- Heat the oil and butter in a wide, heavy-based pan, then fry the onions over a medium heat for 25–30 minutes, stirring frequently to avoid sticking.
- Add the garlic and thyme, then fry for 2–3 minutes. Add the port or marsala and continue to cook until the liquid has reduced by half.
- Add the hot stock, then cover and simmer for 20 minutes.
- While the soup is cooking, make the goats' cheese toasts ... ensure your bread slices fit into your soup bowls and that the goats' cheese log is the same width as the bread (if it's not then crumble the goats' cheese rather than slicing it).
- Lightly toast the bread on both sides and place a slice of goats' cheese onto each toast.
- Continue to grill until the cheese has started to melt and take on some colour.
- Season the soup to taste, then serve with the goats' cheese toasts on top.

Serrano Ham & Broad Bean

Our soup inventing genius, Stacey Howe, came back from a holiday in Barcelona with some impressive salsa skills and a taste for tapas. Her favourite – baby broad beans and *jamón serrano* – is a classic tapas dish which she also found as a soup. She now serves it for special autumn dinner parties and shows off her authenticity by serving it in a ceramic carafe – with a full-bodied Spanish red wine.

It's worth finding Serrano ham from your deli for its depth of colour and flavour. The ham is naturally salty so don't add more without tasting.

Serves 6

Cooking time: 25 minutes

100g Serrano ham (or Parma ham), finely diced
3 tablespoons olive oil
1 medium onion, diced
2 cloves garlic, sliced
200g peas, fresh or defrosted
500g broad beans, podded
1 litre chicken stock
1 bay leaf
1 tablespoon flat leaf parsley, chopped

To garnish ...
70g Serrano ham, cut into fine slivers
250g broad beans

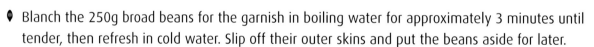

- Blanch the 250g broad beans for the garnish in boiling water for approximately 3 minutes until tender, then refresh in cold water. Slip off their outer skins and put the beans aside for later.
- Heat the olive oil in a pan, add the onion and fry gently for 10 minutes until softened.
- Add the garlic, bay leaf and Serrano ham, then fry for 2–3 minutes. Add the peas and broad beans and stir to heat through.
- Add the hot stock, quickly bring to the boil and simmer for 3 minutes until the peas and broad beans are tender.
- Remove from the heat, add the parsley, then blend in batches until smooth. Reheat and season to taste with pepper only.
- To serve: place a small pile of the broad beans we reserved earlier in each bowl, then top with the slivers of Serrano ham. Pour the soup at the table in front of your guests, then drizzle with olive oil.

Butternut Squash, Chilli & Ginger

For many of us, colour is an important part of dinner party planning. This luxurious soup impresses from the start with a rich autumnal colour set off by cream and coriander. But that's only the start of the sensual experience of eating this delicious soup with its velvety texture, gorgeous aroma and spicy taste.

This is a rich soup so a small espresso cup will be enough for most. For the ultimate in style, make sure you choose crockery and napkins for colour coordination.

Cooking time: 35 minutes

Serves 6

1 large butternut squash, peeled, de-seeded and diced
2 onions, diced
2 cloves garlic, crushed
50g butter
1 tablespoon olive oil
1 red chilli, finely diced
50g sachet creamed coconut
900ml vegetable stock
Coriander leaves to garnish

- Heat the oil and butter in a pan, then over a medium heat sweat the butternut squash, onion and garlic for 5 minutes.
- Add the chilli and ginger, then cook for a further 5 minutes.
- Add the hot stock, bring to the boil, then cover and simmer for 15–20 minutes until the butternut squash is soft.
- Blend in batches until smooth.
- Reheat gently before adding the coconut cream. Season to taste and serve garnished with a few coriander leaves.

Mussel, Fennel & Saffron

One of the joys of approaching winter is the arrival of the season for fresh mussels. Once there is an R in the month, you can make this a highlight of a special seafood dinner. It's well worth making a visit to your fishmonger and taking advice to make sure you have just the right mussels.

This is a sensory food experience: smooth, rich and creamy, with saffron adding extra interest to a subtle blend of flavours. But it's surprisingly light and a wonderful start to a special dinner.

Cooking time: 35 minutes

Serves 6

1kg fresh mussels
200ml dry white wine
2 tablespoons olive oil
25g butter
1 medium carrot, peeled and diced
1 leek, diced
half medium fennel bulb, diced
2 cloves garlic, crushed
1 sprig of thyme
good pinch of saffron
4 medium vine tomatoes, chopped
200ml double cream
500ml fish stock
1 tablespoon parsley, chopped

- Heat the wine in a pan, then add the mussels and cover with a tight fitting lid. Heat for 5–7 minutes, shaking occasionally until the mussels open.
- Drain into a colander set over a bowl (to catch the mussel liquor). Let the mussels cool slightly before removing ¾ of the mussels from their shells.
- Heat the butter and oil in a pan, then add the carrot, leek, fennel and garlic. Cover and cook for 5–10 minutes until softened.
- Gently pour the mussel liquor into a jug, leaving behind any sediment, then make up to 750ml using the fish stock.
- Add the stock, tomatoes, thyme and saffron to the pan, stir, then cover and simmer gently for 20 minutes.
- Remove the thyme, blend then pass through a sieve.
- Rinse out the pan, return it to the heat, then add the cream and mussels before reheating.
- Serve, ensuring you have a good portion of mussels in each bowl, then garnish with the mussels in their shells and parsley.

Steak & Ale

Our soup experts call this Dad Soup. It's ideal for an impromptu visit from the parents – something traditional for Dad who perhaps doesn't always appreciate your more creative continental efforts. What could be more traditional than steak and ale?

It doesn't take too long to prepare and, once the rich warming flavours are bubbling away in the pot, you have time to catch up with the family news. If you can find it, a ruby ale gives extra colour to the gravy. Serve with fluffy mash or a pastry lid and more of the beer.

Serves 6   Cooking time: 2 hours 30 minutes

1kg braising steak, cut into 4cm cubes
200g button mushrooms, whole
2 large onions, finely diced
2 cloves garlic, crushed
4–5 sprigs of thyme
2 bay leaves
2 tablespoons flour
4 tablespoons olive oil
600ml ruby or pale ale

- In a heavy-based pan or casserole dish, fry 1–2 tablespoons of olive oil with the onions over a medium heat for 10 minutes until the onions have softened and taken on some colour.
- Add the garlic and mushrooms, then cook for 5 minutes. Transfer to a dish and set to one side.
- Reheat the casserole dish and brown off the beef in batches using the remaining oil.
- Once all the beef is browned, return it to the pan, then sprinkle over the flour, stir and cook for 2 minutes.
- Add the onions, mushrooms and ale, scraping the base of the pan to retain all the flour and juices. Add the bay leaves and thyme, bring back to a simmer. Cover and allow to simmer gently for 1½ hours.
- Stir the stew and cook for a further 30 minutes, either partially covered or without the lid, depending on the consistency you prefer.
- Remove the thyme and bay leaves, season to taste and serve.

Fish Stew

Whenever Stephen Hill, who has the task of buying all the ingredients our chefs demand, visits his family in Canada, we eagerly await his return with his new recipe ideas. This one will delight all seafood lovers, with an interesting selection of fresh and smoked fish giving a mixture of tastes and textures in a light but creamy sauce.

The tomatoes and herbs added at the last minute give extra colour and a wonderfully fresh taste. Lots of crusty bread to mop up the sauces makes it a satisfying supper dish that is great for a group of friends after a day out in the country.

Serves 6

Cooking time: 50 minutes

200g salmon fillet, cut into chunky 5cm cubes
200g skinned smoked haddock fillet, cut into chunky 5cm cubes
100g scallops, cleaned and shelled (halved if large)
40g butter
2 medium onions, diced
1 tablespoon plain flour
300ml fish stock
120ml white wine
120ml double cream
40g Parmesan cheese, grated
275g fresh tomatoes
small bunch fresh basil, roughly chopped
small bunch fresh parsley, roughly chopped
125g cooked king prawns, peeled

- Preheat your oven to 140°C/275°F/gas mark 1. Meanwhile, melt the butter in a casserole dish, stir in the onion and cook for 10 minutes until soft and golden.
- Add the flour and mix for 1 minute, then stir in the fish stock, cream and wine. Whisk while it comes to the boil.
- Transfer to the oven for 10 minutes, then stir in the Parmesan cheese and season to taste.
- Place the salmon and haddock chunks in a single layer in an ovenproof dish, then pour over the stock mix and cover with foil.
- Increase the oven to 180°C/350°F/gas mark 4 and cook for 15 minutes. Add the scallops and cook for a further 10–15 minutes.
- Meanwhile, drop the tomatoes in a bowl of boiling water for 30 seconds, drain, then peel away the skins. Remove the seeds and cut into chunky strips.
- Remove the dish from the oven, stir in the prawns, tomatoes and fresh herbs, then season to taste.
- Warm through for 2–3 minutes and serve.

Beef Stroganoff

This is another meaty dish so traditional that you could call it retro. Nick Munby, guardian of our good name, likes to entertain with stroganoff because it reminds him of family supper parties in his youth. He serves it as a good sharing meal, in a large pot in the centre of the table, with individual ramekins of basmati rice.

Using fillet steak makes this a quick supper that can be put together after work. You can use rump steak for economy, but the cooking time will need to be increased. The flavour is delicate and ideal for those who like to avoid strong-tasting food. However, other guests might want to add Worcestershire sauce or a little more paprika.

Serves 6

Cooking time: 25 minutes

750g fillet steak, cut into thin slivers
2 medium onions, finely sliced
1 clove garlic, finely sliced
400g chestnut mushrooms, finely sliced
3 tablespoons brandy
3 x 142ml tubs soured cream
3 tablespoons lemon juice
50g butter
4 tablespoons sunflower oil
Worcestershire sauce, to taste
1–2 teaspoons paprika
1–2 tablespoons fresh parsley, chopped

- Heat a large heavy-bottomed frying pan over a medium heat, then add the butter and 2 tablespoons of oil. Add the onions and fry for 5–10 minutes until soft.
- Add the mushrooms and fry quickly until tender. Pour into a dish and set aside.
- Heat the pan until hot, add a little oil, then fry the steak in batches over a high heat until lightly browned.
- Return all the steak to the pan, add the brandy and stir to combine the pan juices and cook off the alcohol.
- Return the mushrooms and onions to the pan, then add the soured cream, lemon juice, seasoning and paprika.
- Heat gently and serve sprinkled with a little more paprika and parsley.

Lamb Tagine

This wonderful fusion of flavours from North Africa gives you something different for an informal supper party. The intriguing tastes and aromas from the fruits and spices are surprisingly easy to achieve. A tagine is a traditionally shaped casserole dish but any large casserole dish will do.

A long simmer is needed for really tender lamb so cooking the night before is a good idea; this will also bring out the flavours even more. Complete the Moroccan theme by serving with couscous or flat bread.

Serves 6

Cooking time: 2 hours

1kg lamb leg steaks, cut into 3cm cubes
5 tablespoons olive oil
2 onions, finely sliced
3 cloves garlic, crushed
1 teaspoon ground cinnamon
1 teaspoon ground cumin
1 teaspoon ground ginger
2 bay leaves
1 x 410g tin of chick peas, drained and rinsed
500ml lamb stock
1 x 400g tin of chopped tomatoes
3 tablespoons fresh coriander, chopped
250g prunes, quartered
1 tablespoon flour
1 teaspoon chilli powder
1 teaspoon ground coriander

- Heat 3 tablespoons of oil in a large casserole dish over a medium heat, then add the onions and cook for 5–10 minutes until softened.
- Add the garlic, cinnamon, cumin, ginger, chilli and coriander and stir for 1–2 minutes. Remove from the pan and set aside.
- In the remaining oil, brown the lamb in batches over a high heat. Add the meat back to the pan with the spicy onions, then sprinkle the flour over the meat and stir for 1–2 minutes.
- Add the tomatoes, bay leaves, chick peas, prunes and stock, then scrape the bottom of the pan to prevent sticking. Bring to a simmer, before covering and cooking on a very low heat for approximately 1½ hours until the lamb is very tender.
- Season to taste and serve.

Seafood Paella

We've stretched the definition of soup even further to include this Spanish favourite, but it is as quick to prepare as a soup and, served in one pot, leaves little mess to clean up. With a bit of planning you can make this colourful dish while your guests are on their way to you or still in the bar round the corner.

This makes a wonderful centre to a table – with vibrant yellows, reds and greens. It's worth taking time to find the authentic ingredients: smoky roasted peppers called *pimientos del piquillo* and *Calasparra* rice from Andalusia. Serve with lemon wedges, green salad and crusty bread.

Serves 6

Cooking time: 35 minutes

- 200g fresh mussels, cleaned and de-bearded
- 400g Calasparra or paella rice, rinsed in cold water
- 1 large onion, finely chopped
- 2 cloves garlic, finely chopped
- large pinch saffron strands, soaked in 150ml of boiling water
- half teaspoon sweet smoked paprika
- 100g pimientos del piquillo (flame roasted peppers in a jar), cut into fine strips
- 400g seafood selection (prawns, mussels, squid rings), fresh or frozen (defrosted if frozen)
- 200g monkfish tail, cut into 3cm chunks
- 12 raw tiger prawns complete with tail section
- 100g peas, fresh or frozen
- 4 vine tomatoes, skinned, de-seeded and chopped
- 200ml dry white wine
- 800ml fish stock
- 5 tablespoons olive oil
- 3 tablespoons parsley, chopped
- 1 lemon, cut into wedges

- Heat 3 tablespoons of olive oil in a large heavy-based frying pan, then add the onion, garlic and peppers. Fry gently for 15 minutes until very soft. Stir in the rice and cook for 2–3 minutes until translucent, then pour in the wine and stir until almost evaporated.
- Add most of the stock, smoked paprika, saffron infusion and tomatoes and cook for 10 minutes, stirring occasionally.
- Add the mussels in their shells, the seafood selection and peas, then stir, adding more stock if necessary.
- In a separate frying pan, heat the remaining oil and fry the monkfish for 2 minutes. Add the prawns and cook for a further 2 minutes until the prawns are pink.
- Transfer to the paella pan, season and check that the rice is cooked; if not, add a little more boiling water and cook for a few minutes longer.
- Remove any un-opened mussels, sprinkle with parsley and serve.

Chilli Con Carne

This is 'blokes' food', much favoured by Mike Cassidy, who ensures our soups hit the shelves. He has a group of mates who are big fans of spaghetti westerns, so he needs a good filling meal to accompany their marathon DVD watching sessions. Fortunately it's everyone's favourite, so Mike makes huge quantities and freezes it in batches.

Steak rather than the usual mince gives this chilli a chunkiness that any strong, slow-speaking screen hero would appreciate.

Mike serves with nachos, guacamole, soured cream, cheddar cheese to sprinkle on top and, of course, beer.

Serves 6 — Cooking time: 2 hours 10 minutes

800g braising steak, cut into 1-2cm chunks
5 tablespoons olive oil
2 medium onions, finely diced
3 green chillies, finely diced
1 teaspoon ground coriander
1 teaspoon ground cumin
2 cardamom pods, bruised with a knife
1 red pepper, finely diced
1 x 400g tin of chopped tomatoes
300ml beef stock
30g dark chocolate, broken into chunks
2 cloves garlic, crushed
1 x 400g tin of red kidney beans, drained and rinsed
1 teaspoon ground cinnamon

- Heat 3 tablespoons of oil in a large pan, add the onions and garlic, then cook gently for 10 minutes until softened.
- Add the chilli, coriander, cumin, cinnamon and cardamom pods and stir gently. Add the red pepper before cooking for a further 5 minutes. Pour into a bowl and set aside.
- Return the pan to a high heat and, using the remaining oil, brown the steak in batches.
- Return all the steak to the pan, add the spicy onions, tomatoes, red kidney beans and stock, then partially cover and simmer over a low heat for 1½ hours until the meat is really tender.
- Add the chocolate and stir until melted, then season to taste and serve.

Minestrone

It seems that everyone here has their own idea of what should be in minestrone. We had a lot of debate before settling on this slightly different recipe, with dark cabbage to add visual drama. It's a hearty winter soup – with beans and pasta which make it a satisfying complete meal – ideal to have ready to warm up for friends or family after an evening out.

When we serve it, the debate about ingredients continues. The basic soup is fine for vegetarians, but others like to add cooked pork, crispy pancetta or a variety of cheeses. So we just put the bowl in the middle of the table surrounded by the other ingredients, chunks of rustic bread and olive oil and let them get on with it.

Serves 6

Cooking time: 1 hour

1 x 400g tin of chopped tomatoes
1 x 410g tin of cannellini beans
2 tablespoons olive oil
2 medium carrots, diced
2 celery sticks, chopped
1 clove garlic, finely sliced
200g swiss chard, savoy cabbage or cavolo nero, cored and shredded
    (ensure the shreds are not too long for ease of eating)
1 litre to 1.5 litres stock
1 dessertspoon fresh thyme, chopped
1 dessertspoon fresh rosemary, chopped
1 leek, diced
2 red onions, diced
75g small pasta shapes (we use conchiglie)

- Heat the olive oil in a heavy pan, then add the carrots, onions, leek, celery, thyme, rosemary and garlic. Cover and sweat without browning over a medium heat for 15 minutes until tender.
- Add the tomatoes and cook for 5 minutes until the juice has reduced slightly.
- Add the stock and cannellini beans, then bring to the boil and simmer for a further 15 minutes. Skim off any red froth if necessary.
- Add the swiss chard and pasta, then simmer for a further 5–10 minutes (the cabbage should retain its dark green colour). Season to taste.
- Adjust the consistency of your soup according to your taste (it should be quite thick), then serve drizzled with olive oil and plenty of grated parmesan.

Sweet Potato, Cauliflower & Spinach Dhal

Supper parties can be difficult if you or some of your guests are slimming. Forget the lettuce leaf and go for this quick and easy dhal, which is low in fat but full of flavour and pleasantly filling. We were inspired by the veggie curries that make up the cuisine of most of the Indian subcontinent, but use red lentils which are quicker to cook than traditional pulses.

If you fancy a bit more indulgence, use a creamy yogurt instead of low fat and top with onions fried in garlic and coriander. Serve with basmati rice to absorb the spicy flavours.

Serves 6

Cooking time: 35 minutes

1 medium (250g) cauliflower, cut into small florets
235g spinach leaves, washed
1 large onion, finely diced
2 cloves garlic, crushed
2 large sweet potatoes, peeled and cut into 2cm dice
1 teaspoon ground cumin
1 teaspoon ground coriander
1 teaspoon turmeric
1 teaspoon hot chilli powder
1 bay leaf
2cm piece root ginger, peeled and grated
900ml vegetable stock
250g red lentils
1 lemon, cut into wedges
20g fresh coriander, chopped
200g low fat yogurt
1 tablespoon olive oil

- Heat the oil in a pan, then fry the onions over a medium heat for 5–10 minutes. Add the garlic, spices and ginger and fry for a further 2–3 minutes to release the aromatic flavours.
- Add the lentils and hot stock, stir, then scrape the base of the pan to amalgamate the spices.
- Add the sweet potato, cauliflower and bay leaf, bring to the boil, then cover and simmer gently for 15 minutes.
- Stir in the spinach carefully to avoid breaking up the other vegetables, cover and cook for a further 3–5 minutes to wilt the spinach. Season to taste, then serve.

Chocolate Fondue with Fruit Skewers

This is a wonderful way to keep chocoholics amused. It's the favourite of our Sue Evans, who makes sure we say the right things on the packs. With her technical background, she claims she uses this recipe to count towards her 5-a-day. We know that it's the quick preparation that really appeals as it means she isn't stuck in the kitchen while the gossip flows at her girlie suppers.

The rich indulgence of the chocolate, cream and brandy are beautifully set off by the fresh fruit that makes her guests feel better about their diets. Sue invites the girls to choose their favourites from strawberries, bananas, nectarines, blackberries, kiwi and pineapple.

Serves 6

Cooking time: 15 minutes

200g plain chocolate (with a high cocoa content), broken into small pieces
200ml single cream
4 tablespoons brandy

Fruit kebabs to serve

- Make your fondue in a glass bowl that fits snugly on the top of a pan (to make a bain marie).
- Fill your pan a third full of water, then bring to the boil.
- Place the chocolate and the cream in the glass bowl, sit the bowl on top of the pan, then stir gently until the chocolate has melted and mixed in with the cream. Make sure the mixture does not overheat.
- Stir in the brandy, then pour into a chocolate fondue set or individual ramekins.
- Serve immediately with your fruit kebabs.

Baked Rhubarb with Orange & Ginger

Debbie Bonnington, who keeps our consumers happy, hails from Leeds near the famed Rhubarb Triangle. This is nothing to do with mysterious disappearances, but it is that bit of West Yorkshire where they force rhubarb for extra tenderness (apparently a good supply of soot is important). Debbie, who grew up munching on rhubarb grown in her parents' garden, introduced us to this chunky fruit soup with a ginger kick.

Our experts say that baking the rhubarb is essential so that it retains its texture. Debbie serves this scrumptious dessert with shortbread and vanilla ice cream.

Serves 6

Cooking time: 40 minutes

1kg rhubarb, washed, trimmed and cut into pieces

150g-200g caster sugar

3 oranges (you need the juice of 3 and the zest of 2)

2cm piece root ginger

- Preheat your oven to 180°C/350°F/gas mark 4.
- Place the rhubarb in a shallow ovenproof dish, sprinkle with sugar, orange zest and ginger, then pour over the orange juice.
- Stir gently, cover with foil then bake for 30 minutes.
- Remove the foil and bake for a further 10 minutes or until the rhubarb is tender but not broken down.
- Leave to cool slightly and serve warm.

Apricot Vodka Granita Cocktail

Is it a soup or a sorbet? Either way, it's gently alcoholic and quite delicious. It makes a cooling dessert on a hot summer's evening, or a palette refresher after a good spicy main course.

When we want to leave our guests 'shaken not stirred', we serve in chilled martini glasses. Cocktail umbrellas or pink swizzle sticks can be used at your discretion.

Serves 6

Cooking time: 25 minutes, plus freezing

400g apricots, halved and stoned
6 tablespoons caster sugar
300ml water

To make the syrup ...
300ml water
125g caster sugar
1 lemon, juice and zest of
60ml vodka

- Place the sugar, water, and apricots in a pan, then gently bring to the boil, ensuring that the sugar has melted.
- Cover and simmer gently for 10–15 minutes until the apricots are cooked.
- Allow to cool a little, then sieve using the back of a ladle to push through as much of the puree as possible. Allow to cool once again.
- To make the syrup, heat the water, sugar and lemon in a pan to dissolve the sugar, bring to the boil and allow to boil for 4 minutes. Leave to cool completely then strain and stir in the apricot puree.
- Add the vodka and stir well.
- Pour into a wide plastic container and put in the freezer. After 2 hours fork the ice crystals which will have formed around the edge into the middle, then re-freeze.
- Repeat the above step every hour or so for around 6 hours until you have an icy, grainy granita with ice crystals in. (You could alternatively leave it in the freezer overnight, thaw for half an hour then fork through.)
- Serve immediately in martini or cocktail glasses.

Blueberry Fool

You might think that the fool is the guest who thinks you took ages to make this fresh fruity concoction. But we're told that the word 'fool' in fruit puddings comes from the French word *fouler* – to crush. Before the days of blenders, fruit had to be crushed through a sieve. Although fool making is now quick and easy, the boiled fruit is still best sieved for ultimate smoothness.

This colourful dessert soup, with its ripples of folded cream, looks quite beautiful served in individual glasses.

Serves 6 *Cooking time: 30 minutes, plus chilling time*

275g blueberries
1 tablespoon caster sugar
550ml double cream

- Place 150g of the blueberries in a pan, then add the sugar and 2 tablespoons of water. Bring to the boil and simmer for 5 minutes. Leave to cool.
- Blend the cooled blueberries and sieve to make a coulis. Place in the refrigerator to chill.
- Meanwhile, whip the cream until it holds its peaks but is not over whipped. Fold in the remaining blueberries and chill.
- When you are ready to serve your fool, pour the coulis into the cream mixture and fold gently twice over to ripple the mixture.
- Spoon into glasses and serve either on its own or with thin almond biscuits.

Soups for Out & About

Al Fresco   Days Out   Lunchboxes

Soups for Out & About

However you enjoy yourself outdoors, here are soups that will impress, sustain and satisfy your family and friends.

For *al fresco* dining on the patio, balcony or picnic rug, we have new recipes with garden-fresh flavours, bright colours or memories of holiday eating. Some are designed for the start of a stylish garden party; others are ideal for friends or family after a day enjoying the outdoors.

Soup is wonderfully portable. With a flask and a cup you're set up for a day out. We have soups for tramping over hills, standing on touchlines or enjoying posh sporting picnics.

Forget the tired sandwich or the repetitive pork pie, pack a soup in your lunchbox. It will almost certainly be healthier and more stimulating – even making healthy eating fun for children. You'll be the envy of friends and colleagues and you can keep ringing the changes with new recipes.

Most of these can be made ahead in batches, or the night before so that you're ready to set out and enjoy yourself.

Don't leave home without a soup.

Yogurt, Cucumber & Mint

Jeremy Hudson, our financial wizard, is famous for his barbecues in the back garden. At the moment he is on a Greek kick and conjures up the cuisine of his favourite holiday destination in the Aegean. Small bowls of this light and refreshing soup fit in brilliantly.

The tzatziki-like flavours complement the spicy meats that he loves so much. And when his barbecues are rewarded with Mediterranean weather, a chilled palette cleanser is very welcome.

Serves 8 — Cooking time: 10 minutes plus chilling time

3 large cucumbers
1 clove garlic, crushed
500ml Greek yogurt
250ml single cream
1 lemon, juice of
600ml chicken stock
4 spring onions, chopped
2 tablespoons fresh mint, chopped
10g fresh dill, chopped
Tabasco, to taste

- Take half of one of the cucumbers, de-seed and dice, then put aside for the garnish.
- Peel, de-seed and roughly chop the remaining cucumbers, then place in a blender with all the other ingredients except the mint, dill and Tabasco.
- Blend until smooth, then chill for 3–4 hours.
- When you are ready to serve, check the seasoning, add the Tabasco as required, then serve garnished with the set-aside cucumber, mint and dill.

Summer Vegetable & Pesto

Alison Robertson, who is in charge of all things technical, has always particularly loved garden-fresh vegetables. Because her idea of gardening has more to do with deckchairs than double digging, she is a regular at her local farm shop.

The quick simmer makes sure that the vibrant green colours and subtle flavours of the vegetables are preserved. It also gives Alison a little more relaxation time before she serves this to an admiring audience.

Serves 8

Cooking time: 20 minutes

100g green beans, sliced into 2cm lengths
175g podded broad beans
120g podded peas
2 tablespoons olive oil
2 cloves garlic, peeled and crushed
1 onion, finely chopped
3 courgettes, diced
2 sticks celery, finely diced
1.5 litres vegetable stock
1 tablespoon fresh basil, finely shredded
1 tablespoon fresh mint, finely shredded
50g parmesan, finely grated
3 tablespoons fresh pesto

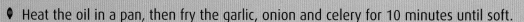

- Heat the oil in a pan, then fry the garlic, onion and celery for 10 minutes until soft.
- Add the courgettes and chicken stock, then bring to the boil, cover and simmer for 5 minutes.
- Add the peas, green beans and broad beans and simmer for a further 5 minutes.
- Remove from the heat and stir in the basil and mint.
- Serve topped with parmesan and drizzled with pesto, along with lots of crusty bread.

Gazpacho

In the heat of Andalusia, this cool soup has many local variations. This is our favourite version as it really brings out the flavour of the sweet tomatoes. The secret is in finding the best olive oil and red wine vinegar – well worth an hour at the local market if you're in Spain.

At home, all you need is some quick work with the food processor and it can chill away while you prepare the rest of the meal. To eat in true Spanish style, serve with crushed ice, a colourful choice of garnishes and a dash of Tabasco for your guests to add themselves. For complete authenticity, try some Flamenco dancing – or just play the music if you're not brave enough.

Serves 8
Cooking time: 10 minutes plus chilling time

4 cloves garlic
1.3kg sweet ripe tomatoes
1 red pepper, de-seeded and finely chopped
1 yellow pepper, de-seeded and finely chopped
1 small red onion, finely diced
75g ciabatta, crusts removed and cubed
4 tablespoons red wine vinegar
5 tablespoons olive oil
250ml tomato juice

To garnish ...
Croutons (for great croutons see our Garnishes section)
Diced tomato, pepper and cucumber
Fresh basil, torn

- Crush the garlic to a smooth paste with a little salt, either using the back of a knife or a pestle and mortar.
- Blend all of the ingredients, except the tomato juice, until smooth.
- Sieve half the soup to give it a finer texture, then stir into the remaining half and add the tomato juice. Stir once again before chilling well.
- When the soup has chilled and you are ready to serve, adjust the seasoning with salt and pepper, adding a little more olive oil and red wine vinegar to taste. You could also add some Tabasco at this stage too.
- Serve chilled with a little crushed ice piled in the middle of the soup.

Kitchen Herb Garden

When Claire Francis, who helps develop our new food ideas, moved from the country to the city, she couldn't quite leave behind her passion for growing her own. So now she has the greenest urban window box bursting with fresh garden herbs.

You can experiment with ingredients from your herb garden, but this is Claire's favourite combination, making a wonderfully scented soup with added bite from the crunchy baby gem lettuce. Serve on the patio or with the windows open to enjoy the evening aroma of the herb garden.

Serves 8

Cooking time: 30 minutes

200g fresh peas
500g potatoes, peeled and diced
50g butter
8 spring onions, sliced
2 cloves garlic, crushed
1.5 litres vegetable stock
3 baby gem lettuces, finely sliced
2 tablespoons fresh parsley, chopped
2 tablespoons fresh thyme, chopped
2 tablespoons fresh chives, chopped
2 tablespoons fresh mint, chopped
2 tablespoons fresh tarragon, chopped
200ml single cream
Half lemon, juice of

- Melt the butter in a pan, add the spring onion, garlic and potato, cover, then sweat for 10 minutes.
- Add the stock and bring to the boil. Cover and cook for 15 minutes.
- Add half the lettuce and herbs and cook for a further 3–5 minutes.
- Blend, then add the remaining lettuce, cream and lemon juice. Reserve a few herbs for garnishing, then add the rest to the pan. Heat through gently and serve.

Melon & Mint

On a warm evening, with the heat of the day still coming off the patio, you'll invoke memories of Mediterranean holidays when you start an evening with this elegant and impressive soup.

The floating melon and mint make this look as good as it tastes. For a little extra style, serve in glasses accompanied by Parma ham and breadsticks to nibble. A chilled rosé completes the holiday feeling.

Serves 8

Time: 20 minutes plus chilling

3 Charentais melons
2 Galia melons
2 lemons, juice of
150ml grape juice
150ml dry white wine
2-3 sprigs fresh mint leaves, shredded
Crushed ice

- Cut the melons in half, and scoop out the seeds over a bowl to catch any juices.
- Using a melon baller, scoop out 48 melon balls and set to one side.
- Remove the rest of the flesh from the melons then blend together (you may need to do this in batches) with the wine, grape juice and lemon juice.
- Blend until smooth, then chill well.
- To serve, garnish each bowl with 6 melon balls, a few shredded mint leaves and some crushed ice.

Parsley Soup

We have a surprising number of parsley enthusiasts here at New Covent Garden Food Co. who have been demanding that we pay proper attention to their favourite herb. Their lobbying has been successful as our kitchen has created a soup that makes parsley the star.

The light flavour is a wonderful prelude to fish dishes, while the bright green colour sets off the table beautifully. The only problem is what to use as a garnish: a swirl of crème fraîche looks great, but perhaps the enthusiasts would demand more parsley.

Serves 8

Cooking time: 25 minutes

4 large leeks, sliced
600g potatoes, peeled and diced
1.5 litres vegetable stock
100g butter
300g fresh parsley
150ml crème fraîche
1 whole nutmeg, grated

- Wash the parsley well, then separate the stalks and leaves. Roughly chop all the stalks and half the leaves.
- Melt the butter in a pan, add the leeks and cook gently for 5 minutes.
- Add the parsley stalks and chopped leaves, along with the potatoes and stock. Bring to the boil, cover and simmer for 15–20 minutes.
- Add the remaining parsley leaves, then simmer for a further 2 minutes before removing from the heat.
- Blend the soup in batches, then reheat gently while stirring in the crème fraîche. Add the grated nutmeg, season to taste and serve.

Roasted Red Pepper, Goats' Cheese & Rocket

What a way to start an *al fresco* party! As the large red sun sinks towards the horizon on a summer evening, serve this delicious red soup in white bowls on white linen. The classic summer flavours and gentle heat from the paprika will give your guests a warm glow to carry through the evening.

The rich colour of the soup is best set off by the dark green rocket and a generous dollop of goats' cheese. And, of course, it tastes as good as it looks.

Serves 8

Cooking time: 1 hour

8 large red peppers
1.5 litres vegetable stock
2 medium onions, finely chopped
2 carrots, peeled and diced
2 sticks celery, diced
1 head garlic
3 tablespoons olive oil
1 teaspoon sweet smoked paprika
150g soft goats' cheese
50g rocket leaves

- Pre-heat your oven to 230°C/ 450°F/gas mark 8.
- Cut the peppers in half, removing the seeds but leaving the stalks intact, then place in a roasting tin as a single layer with the skins facing upwards.
- Wrap the garlic head in foil, add to the tin, then roast for 30 minutes until the pepper skins are lightly charred.
- Place the peppers in a bowl, cover with cling film and allow to cool. Once cooled, the skins should be easy to remove.
- Meanwhile, heat the oil in a pan, add the onions, carrots and celery, then cover and cook for 15–20 minutes until softened. Add the smoked paprika and stir.
- Add the stock and skinless peppers (as well as their juices) to the pan.
- Squeeze half of the roasted garlic cloves from their skins and add to the pan (you can use the other half in a bruschetta or pasta dish), bring to the boil and remove from the heat.
- Blend in batches, season to taste and serve with a small handful of rocket leaves and crumbled goats' cheese.

Salsa Soup

We created this from the flavours of our favourite dip. Putting the fresh taste of plump juicy tomatoes into a colourful soup, this is a great way to fire up a barbecue.

There's a lot of Mexican heritage here. Mexicans enjoy grilled corn as a popular street food. You can cook corn on the barbecue and serve with tortilla chips, shredded chicken, grated cheese and soured cream for a filling first course. Served cold this is a brilliant addition to the picnic basket.

Cooking time: 45 minutes

Serves 8

For the soup ...
2 x 400g tins chopped tomatoes
2 cloves garlic, crushed
2 tablespoons olive oil
1 tablespoon fresh basil, chopped
Half red pepper, de-seeded and finely diced

Salsa garnish ...
450g plum tomatoes
140g cherry vine tomatoes, halved
1 small red onion, finely diced
2 red chillies, de-seeded and finely diced
1 lime, juice of
2 tablespoons olive oil
20g fresh coriander, chopped
Half red pepper, de-seeded and diced
2 corn cobs

- Place all the soup ingredients in a pan, bring to the boil and simmer for 20 minutes.
- Meanwhile, prepare the salsa ... plunge the plum tomatoes into boiling water for approximately 30 seconds, then peel, de-seed and dice. Place in a large bowl.
- Add the cherry tomato halves to the bowl, then add all the other salsa ingredients except for the corn cobs. Set the bowl aside and allow to marinate for at least 30 minutes.
- Heat your grill on a high setting, brush the corn cobs lightly with olive oil, then grill until a dark golden colour and slightly charred. You will need to turn them frequently.
- Allow the corn cobs to cool slightly, then cut off all the kernels by holding the cob at one end on a board and slicing down the cob.
- Serve warm or chilled – pour the soup into the bowls, top with a good spoonful of salsa and some of the corn.
- Place bowls of tortilla chips, shredded cooked chicken, grated cheese and soured cream on the table for your guests to help themselves.

Oxtail Soup

This is the ultimate comfort food – the kind of thing that Mum used to give you along with a woolly scarf and an instruction to wrap up warm. Andrew Ovens, our marketing guru, pinched his mum's recipe and always takes along a flask when watching his son's football team.

It not only warms him down to his feet, but also the others he shares it with along the touchline. His soup has such local fame that, when the club is rich enough to build seating, it will probably be known as the Oxtail Stand.

Serves 4

Cooking time: 3 hours, 20 minutes

700g oxtail, cut into pieces (your butcher will do this for you)
3 tablespoons plain flour
3–4 tablespoons olive oil
2 medium carrots, peeled and chopped
2 onions, finely chopped
2 sticks celery, diced
1 tablespoon fresh thyme, chopped
850ml beef stock
300ml red wine
1 bay leaf
1 tablespoon fresh parsley, chopped

- Season the flour with salt and pepper, then lightly coat the oxtail pieces.
- Heat half the oil in a heavy frying pan, then fry the oxtail in batches until browned. Transfer to a casserole dish.
- Preheat your oven to 150°C/300°F/gas mark 2.
- Fry the carrots, onions and celery in the remaining oil until brown, then pour in any remaining seasoned flour to soak up the juices. Scrape the pan to gather up any of the crispy bits at the bottom.
- Add the wine to the pan, stir, then reduce a little. Add the stock and thyme, stir, then bring to a simmer.
- Transfer to the casserole dish, stir well and place in the oven to cook very gently for 2–3 hours.
- Remove the oxtail pieces and fork out the meat, shredding a little if you need to.
- Return the meat to the mixture, blend, then reheat gently, before stirring in the parsley. Serve immediately or pour into a flask to enjoy later.

Chicken, Vegetable & Pearl Barley

When you are planning an autumn family day out, you know that one or two are going to get tired and complain about being cold and bored. This meal in itself will keep the grumbliest tums quiet and help you all enjoy the whole day.

This was chosen as our Soup of the Month for December 2008, with a contribution from every carton sold going to support The Salvation Army's Resettlement Centre programme.

Serves 4

Cooking time: 1 hour

100g cooked chicken, cut into small cubes
1 small leek, chopped
1 small carrot, peeled and chopped
2 waxy new potatoes, peeled and diced
50g peas
1 medium potato, peeled and diced
1 small onion, chopped
1 clove garlic, crushed
1 tablespoon flour
900ml chicken stock
50ml double cream
1 tablespoon fresh parsley, finely chopped
50g pearl barley

- Place the chicken stock, onion, 180g potatoes and garlic in a large pan, bring to the boil, then cover and simmer for approximately 20 minutes until the vegetables are tender.
- Mix the flour with a little water to make a paste, then add to the soup and stir until thickened.
- Blend until smooth before adding the carrots, 50g potatoes and the pearl barley. Cook for 25 minutes.
- Add the leeks and cook for 10 minutes.
- Add the peas and chicken before cooking for a further 5–10 minutes.
- Stir in the cream and parsley, then serve.

Beetroot, Lemon & Chive

The sweet and earthy taste of beetroot is underrated and underused, but this colourful soup is an easy introduction to those who've yet to see the light. Beetroot converts tell us that it has loads of health-giving properties and is the ideal accompaniment to a power walk.

Our recipe team put this together for a New Year's Day recovery stroll. The antioxidants in the beetroot help you to detox after a heavy night. This wonderful vegetable also contains tryptophan (as does chocolate), which aids relaxation to give a sense of well-being.

Serves 4

Cooking time: 50 minutes

500g raw beetroot, peeled and chopped
1 onion, finely chopped
1 carrot, peeled and chopped
1 clove garlic, crushed
1 medium potato, peeled and chopped
Half lemon, juice of
750ml beef stock
1 teaspoon sugar
1 tablespoon fresh chives, chopped
2 tablespoons olive oil

- Heat the oil in a pan, add the carrot, onion, beetroot and garlic, then sweat for 10 minutes until softened.
- Add the stock, sugar and potato, then cover and simmer for 40 minutes until the vegetables are tender.
- Blend until smooth, then stir in the chives. Adjust the seasoning and add the lemon juice and more sugar if necessary (this will depend on how earthy in flavour you like your beetroot).
- Reheat and serve.

Butternut Squash & Parmesan

On an autumn day when the weather clears suddenly, you decide on a family walk. Here's a soup you can put together very quickly while the others argue about where to go. It's full of theflavours of Italian risotto, with a smooth sweet taste that everyone will love as you kick your way through the fallen leaves.

As a seasonal alternative, why not try using pumpkin instead of butternut squash.

Serves 4

Cooking time: 35 minutes

1 medium onion, chopped
25g butter
1 tablespoon olive oil
1 large (900g) butternut squash, peeled, de-seeded and diced
2 cloves garlic, crushed
1 bay leaf
650ml vegetable stock
1 tablespoon lemon juice
30g-40g parmesan, grated

- Heat the butter and oil in a pan, then sweat the onion and butternut squash for 10 minutes, stirring occasionally to prevent it from sticking.
- Add the garlic and cook for a further 5 minutes.
- Add the stock and the bay leaf, bring to the boil and simmer for 15–20 minutes until tender.
- Blend until smooth, add the lemon juice, adjust the seasoning to taste, then add the parmesan.
- Stir, then reheat and serve.

Smoked Haddock & Horseradish

Rob Burnett, our great leader, is a true Scotsman, wearing the kilt and all the trimmings. When he invites friends and family to the ancestral pile, they can look forward to long, healthy walks over heather-clad hills.

To restore his guests, he serves this creamy version of a traditional chowder, using local smoked haddock with a kick of horseradish to blow away the cobwebs. To avoid too many calls from friends feeling the pull of the Highlands, he has allowed the recipe to travel south.

Serves 4

Cooking time: 30 minutes

300g undyed smoked haddock fillets, skinned and diced
1 medium potato, peeled and chopped
25g butter
2 small leeks, sliced
300ml fish stock
300ml milk
1 tablespoon horseradish sauce
1 tablespoon fresh chives, snipped
100ml single cream

- Melt the butter in a pan, add the leeks, cover, then sweat for 10 minutes until softened.
- Add the potatoes, bay leaf, milk and stock. Stir, then cover and simmer gently for 10 minutes.
- Add the smoked haddock and simmer for a further 5 minutes until the haddock is cooked.
- Blend until smooth. Reheat, add the cream, chives and horseradish (we used a tablespoon, but the strength of your horseradish will vary so adjust according to taste).
- Stir before serving or pouring into a flask.

Roasted Chestnut & Truffle Oil

This is a posh out-and-about soup, ideal for a warming picnic from the back of the 4x4, as served by our own point-to-pointer (and technical head), Russell Nearn.

The aroma of roast chestnuts is warming in itself, while the truffle oil gives a rich mushroomy flavour and juniper adds a touch of sophistication. It's a beautifully smooth soup, but Russell adds a bit more stock when serving it from cups to his fellow 'pointers'.

Serves 4

Cooking time: 35 minutes

300g roast chestnuts, ready roasted and vacuum packed
50g butter
1 large onion, finely chopped
1 medium potato, peeled and diced
2 sticks celery, chopped
850ml chicken stock
3 juniper berries, crushed (optional)
2 bay leaves
100ml single cream
2 cloves garlic, chopped
1 dessertspoon truffle oil

- Melt the butter in a pan, add the celery, onion and garlic, then cook for 10 minutes until softened.
- Add the potato, chestnuts, bay leaves and juniper berries and stir.
- Pour over the stock, bring to the boil, then cover and simmer for 15–20 minutes until tender.
- Remove the bay leaves and blend in batches until smooth.
- Return to the pan, add the cream and adjust the seasoning to taste. Add the truffle oil, again to taste, and any additional stock if required.
- Reheat before serving or pouring into a flask.

Indian Spiced Vegetable

On the subcontinent, they spend much more time watching cricket in searing heat than football in English drizzle. However, this Indian-inspired creation is the ideal pitch-side soup. Tuck in when the pre-match beer has worn off and your cold feet are stretching your loyalty to those on the pitch.

The lovely depth of flavour from the roast vegetables and the definite kick from the authentic Indian spices will make even a 0–0 draw into a worthwhile afternoon.

Serves 4

Cooking time: 1 hour

- 150g celeriac, peeled and diced
- 1 parsnip, peeled and diced
- 1 sweet potato, peeled and diced
- 1 carrot, peeled and diced
- 1 small onion, finely chopped
- 1 celery stick, diced
- 1 clove garlic, crushed
- 4 tablespoons olive oil
- 1 teaspoon ground coriander
- 1 teaspoon cumin seeds
- half teaspoon black onion seeds (optional)
- half teaspoon chilli powder
- 850ml vegetable stock

- Preheat your oven to 190°C/375°F/gas mark 5.
- Place the celeriac, carrot, parsnip and sweet potato in a roasting tin and drizzle them with 2 tablespoons of olive oil.
- Sprinkle over all the spices and salt and pepper, then stir to coat all the vegetables.
- Roast for 40 minutes, turning occasionally.
- Meanwhile, heat the remaining olive oil in a pan, add the onion, garlic and celery, then cover and sweat for 15 minutes.
- Add the roasted vegetables and stock, bring to a simmer, then cover and cook for 10 minutes.
- Blend in batches until completely smooth.

Borlotti Bean, Pancetta & Pasta

This is a classic Italian combination that will give you a much-needed energy boost after a stiff hike. It might be a good idea to use a wide-necked flask and put a spoon in your rucksack since it's as chunky as it is filling.

Borlotti beans give a smooth texture and a sweet taste so this is a soup that everyone will enjoy as a meal in itself. The pasta will quickly give you all the energy you need to get back to base.

Cooking time: 25 minutes

Serves 4

1 x 410g tin borlotti beans, rinsed and drained
80g small pasta tubes or macaroni
1 stick celery, finely chopped
1 medium onion, finely diced
1 carrot, finely chopped
140g pancetta cubes
1 tablespoon tomato puree
1 tablespoon fresh rosemary, finely chopped
2 cloves garlic, crushed
1 bay leaf
2 tablespoons olive oil
1 litre chicken stock

- Heat the olive oil in a saucepan, then sweat the onion, carrot, celery and garlic for 10 minutes until softened.
- Add the stock, borlotti beans and bay leaf, then bring to the boil, cover and simmer for 15 minutes.
- Meanwhile, fry the pancetta in a frying pan. Once the fat starts to run, add the rosemary and fry until the pancetta is dark and golden.
- Transfer a quarter of the soup (a couple of ladlefuls) to a bowl, then blend. Return the blended soup to the pan, along with the tomato puree, pasta, pancetta and rosemary. Cover and simmer for a further 10 minutes until the pasta is cooked.
- Check the seasoning and serve.
- We have used tinned borlotti beans here, but if you wish to use dried borlotti beans, simply soak them overnight, then simmer in step 2 for 1 hour (rather than 15 minutes).

Yummy Tomato (for children)

This is a favourite of Dotty's, 5-year-old daughter of our creative designer Michelle Harriman, which she enjoys having when she puts on her pink flowery wellies to visit nearby West Lodge Farm Park to say hello to the pigs and peacocks.

The apple adds the sweetness that Dotty loves. And while Dotty dunks her sandwiches in the scrumptiously coloured soup, Michelle's happy to have slipped a few vegetables into her diet.

Cooking time: 35 minutes

Serves 4

600g tinned tomatoes (one and a half tins)
Half red pepper, de-seeded and diced
Half eating apple, peeled and diced
1 tablespoon olive oil
25g butter
1 small onion, finely diced
1 stick celery, diced
1 carrot, peeled and diced
50ml double cream
500ml vegetable stock

- Heat the oil and butter in a saucepan, then sweat the carrot, onion, pepper and celery for 10–15 minutes until well softened.
- Add the tomatoes and stock before bringing to the boil. Cover and simmer for 10–15 minutes.
- Add the apple, then cover and simmer for a further 5 minutes.
- Leave to cool slightly before blending until completely smooth.
- Re-heat gently, add the cream, then season – remembering it's for the children!
- If you're eating at home you can garnish with home-made croutons. Use cookie cutters to create some great shapes.

Easy Cheesy (for children)

'That's gross, Mum!' said Olly, the rather fussy son of Corinna from our PR team, when presented with cauliflower prepared in the traditional way. So Corinna came up with this nifty way of disguising the goodness of vegetables with his favourite taste – cheese – and keeping his nose out of the biscuit tin.

When Olly brings a few friends home to play after school, Corinna can send them out into the garden with a nourishing, tasty soup and chunky bread to mop up the last drops. In fact, Corinna's garden is becoming a popular place with Olly's gang.

Serves 4

Cooking time: 35 minutes

1 small cauliflower, cut into florets
100–150g cheese, finely grated
50g butter
1 small onion, finely diced
1 medium potato, peeled and diced
700ml vegetable stock
100ml milk

- Melt the butter in a saucepan and sweat the onions for 10 minutes until soft.
- Add the potato and cauliflower, stir, then add the stock.
- Bring to the boil, cover, then simmer for 20 minutes.
- Blend until completely smooth.
- Reheat gently, adding the milk and cheese, then stir until the cheese has melted.
- Serve to a hungry gang and watch with delight as they eat part of their 5-a-day.

Classic Bolognese Soup

Bolognese is hearty, yummy, versatile and portable. So it's perfect for everyone's lunchbox. In fact, our soup tasters have found it so popular that they are having to make big batches for the freezer to keep up with demand.

With added pasta, it's ideal central heating for children on a cold winter's day. With a bit of garlic bread, it will also keep hard-working parents well satisfied whether they are indoors or out.

Serves 4

Cooking time: 2 hours

- 150g beef mince
- 150g pork mince
- 100g pancetta
- 2 tablespoons olive oil
- 1 small onion, finely chopped
- 1 small carrot, peeled and diced
- 1 stick celery, diced
- 2 cloves garlic, crushed
- 1 x 400g tin chopped tomatoes
- 4 tablespoons tomato puree
- 200ml red wine
- 400ml beef stock
- 2 teaspoon dried oregano
- 2 tablespoons fresh basil, shredded

- Heat the oil in a frying pan, then fry the onions, garlic, carrot and celery until soft and browned. Transfer to a saucepan.
- Reheat the frying pan and fry the pancetta until it starts to brown and the fat starts to run.
- Add the beef and pork mince to the frying pan and brown. Then add the wine, reduce a little, and transfer to the saucepan of vegetables.
- Add the tomatoes, oregano, stock and tomato puree to the saucepan, cover, then simmer gently for 1½ hours.
- Add the shredded basil and season to taste, adding a little more stock or water if necessary.
- Sprinkle with parmesan or grated cheese to serve.
- To make a heartier soup, add a handful of small pasta shapes 15 minutes before the end of cooking.

Thai Green Curry

Sometimes you know the working day is going to be unavoidably dull and boring. This spicy taste of the Orient will give you something to look forward to at lunchtime and will carry you through an afternoon that threatens monotony.

The list of ingredients for the paste looks long but they all go in the blender. Why not make bigger amounts and store it? We're sure you'll want to enjoy this soup again and again.

Cooking time: 20 minutes

Serves 4

For the paste ...

- 1 stick lemongrass, chopped
- 2 green Birds Eye chillies, de-seeded and chopped
- 2 shallots, peeled and chopped
- 2 cloves garlic, peeled and chopped
- 1 teaspoon ground cumin
- 1 teaspoon ground coriander
- 1 tablespoon Thai fish sauce
- 1 lime, zest and juice of

2 tablespoons olive oil
1 x 400ml tin coconut milk
2 small chicken breasts, cut into strips
500ml chicken stock
100g Basmati rice, washed before cooking to remove the starch
10g fresh basil, shredded
10g fresh coriander leaves, shredded

- Place all the paste ingredients in a blender and blend to a fine paste.
- Heat the oil in a saucepan, then fry the chicken and paste for 3–4 minutes over a medium heat, taking care as it will spit.
- Add the coconut milk and stock, then bring to a simmer and add the rice.
- Cover and simmer for approximately 7 minutes until the rice is just cooked.
- Sprinkle with the shredded basil and coriander leaves, then serve and enjoy.
- If you are splitting and serving this over a couple of days, you will need to add more stock or water as the rice will continue to absorb the liquid.

Goulash Soup

When Jim Watson, our chief soup maker, came back from his skiing trip in the Austrian Alps, he entertained us with stories of his prowess on the *piste* and brought to work the hearty and warming goulash that kept him going in the hills.

This wonderfully flexible dish has really caught on with us. Not everyone shares Jim's love of adventure so they do without the Tabasco, but others have taken the recipe home to serve as a family meal with soured cream and parsley.

Serves 4

Cooking time: 2 hours 20 minutes

500g braising steak, small cubes
1 large onion, finely chopped
3 tablespoons olive oil
500ml beef stock
2 cloves garlic, crushed
1 teaspoon caraway seeds
2 tablespoons paprika
1 x 400g tin chopped tomatoes
100g new potatoes, cubed
1 tablespoon fresh parsley, chopped
2 tablespoons plain flour
3 tablespoons soured cream
few drops Tabasco

- Coat the braising steak well with seasoned flour.
- Heat a little of the oil in a frying pan, then fry off the steak in batches until nicely browned, setting to one side as you do each batch. Add the stock, then stir to collect pan juices.
- Heat the remaining oil in a large saucepan, fry the onion until softened and golden, add the garlic, caraway seeds and paprika, then fry for a further 2 minutes.
- Add the steak and tomatoes to the saucepan, stir, then add the stock. Bring to a simmer, cover, then simmer gently for 1 hour, stirring occasionally.
- Add the new potatoes and simmer gently for a further 1 hour until the potatoes are cooked and the beef is very tender.
- Check the seasoning, add Tabasco to taste, then stir in the chopped parsley and a dollop of soured cream.

Chickpea, Chilli & Lime

This is a healthy alternative to the lunchtime sandwich. We've found it even goes down well with people who claim not to like chickpeas. There's a lively and warming hint of Morocco in the flavours.

Even better, chickpeas contain slow release carbohydrates so you can avoid the mid-afternoon slump that leaves you staring dispiritedly out of the window – or reaching for a snack you know you don't really need.

Serves 4

Cooking time: 55 minutes

1 x 400g tin chopped tomatoes
1 x 400g tin chickpeas, drained
2 tablespoons olive oil
1 medium onion, finely diced
2 cloves garlic, crushed
2 teaspoons ground cumin
10g fresh coriander, stalks and leaves separated and finely chopped
2 red chillies, de-seeded and finely chopped
half lime, zest and juice of
800ml vegetable stock

- Heat the oil in a large saucepan, then sweat the onion for 5–10 minutes until softened.
- Add the coriander stalks, cumin, chilli and garlic to the saucepan, then stir for a couple of minutes until aromatic.
- Add the tomatoes, cover, then cook over a medium heat for 15 minutes until the tomatoes have thickened.
- Add the chickpeas and stock and bring to the boil, cover and simmer for a further 20 minutes.
- Blend two thirds of the soup (if you prefer a completely smooth soup then blend all of it).
- Return the blended soup to the pan, then add the lime zest, lime juice and coriander leaves.
- Season to taste and serve.

Greek Salad Soup

If you'd really rather be on holiday than at work, conjure up a Greek mood with this summer salad in a soup bowl. The mix of flavours and colours will refresh and restore you and set you up for a dynamic and productive afternoon.

The easiest way to enjoy it in the office is to take the soup and salad separately and assemble it at your desk, with a bread roll to make sure you mop up everything. Your colleagues may be intrigued, and they will certainly be impressed, so you'd better be ready with a copy of the recipe.

Serves 8   **Cooking time: 30 minutes plus chilling**

600g very ripe plum tomatoes, roughly chopped
200g cherry tomatoes
200ml passata
2 teaspoons balsamic vinegar
1 clove garlic, chopped
320g feta cheese, cubed
240g marinated Kalamata olives
1 medium red onion, finely sliced
half large cucumber, peeled, de-seeded, cut into large dice
500g vine tomatoes
150g cherry tomatoes, halved
2 tablespoons fresh oregano, chopped
1 tablespoon flat leaf parsley, roughly chopped
half lemon, juice of

- Blend the plum tomatoes, whole cherry tomatoes, passata, balsamic vinegar and garlic, then sieve and chill.
- Half an hour before serving, make the Greek salad. Put the red onion into a large bowl, then sprinkle over the lemon juice and allow to steep for 5 minutes.
- Cut the vine tomatoes through the middle and cut each half into quarters, then add to the bowl.
- Add the diced cucumber, halved cherry tomatoes and herbs, then stir.
- Pour the chilled tomato soup into bowls, top with Greek salad, then scatter over the olives and cubed feta cheese.
- Drizzle with olive oil and a few extra herbs and serve with crusty bread.

Root Vegetable & Red Lentil

James Bond sells our soups to cafés and restaurants, so he knows a great deal about food. And he has heard every 007 joke going. Because he never quite knows where he will be at lunchtime he often relies on a flask of soup to keep him going.

Although he's not a vegetarian, he's found that this healthy creation keeps him going throughout the day. He's certainly the only secret agent licensed to carry Worcestershire sauce in his glove compartment.

Serves 4

Cooking time: 45 minutes

100g red lentils, rinsed and drained
2 medium leeks, sliced
2 medium carrots, diced
half medium swede, diced
2 medium potatoes, diced
2 parsnips, diced
750ml vegetable stock
50ml milk
2 tablespoons olive oil

- Heat the oil in a large saucepan, then sauté the leeks for 5–10 minutes until softened.
- Add the rest of the vegetables and lentils, stir for a few minutes, then add the stock.
- Bring to the boil, cover and simmer for 30 minutes until all the vegetables are tender.
- Blend, then reheat gently, adding the milk and a little water if necessary to achieve the right consistency.
- Season to taste and serve. This tastes great with a dash of Worcestershire sauce.

Soups for

Calendar Occasions

Valentine's Day   Halloween & Bonfire   Christmas

Soups for Calendar Occasions

When we spot a special occasion coming up on the calendar, many of us like to look for new ways to celebrate it. Whether you are preparing a special meal for two on Valentine's Day or warming a hungry family on bonfire night, you'll be looking for something different.

That's the wonderful versatility of soup: it can easily be adapted for almost any occasion. Here, our chefs have put their heads together and come up with some new creations to help you celebrate.

You'll find ingenious ways to use up the Christmas leftovers, neat ideas for restoring guests who have partied the night before and unusual child-pleasers like Bangers & Creamy Mash soup.

A soup can be an easy but impressive way to begin a special occasion dinner or the centrepiece of a feast for bigger gatherings of family and friends. We hope you have as much fun making and serving these recipes as we did creating them.

Crushed Velvet
Wild Mushroom drizzled with Truffle Oil

When you want to show you really care, a touch of opulence and hand-made croutons will certainly do the trick. The truffle oil in this recipe has that hint of decadence and speaks of no expense spared.

Top the velvety texture and delicate flavours with heart-shaped croutons that show the special effort you've made and your loved one will feel they are the most important person in the world.

Serves 2

Cooking time: 40 minutes

15g dried porcini mushrooms
3 shallots, thinly sliced
1 clove garlic, crushed
2 teaspoons fresh thyme, finely chopped
25g butter
1 tablespoon olive oil
250g mixed mushrooms (chestnut, chanterelle, girolle), cleaned and sliced
250ml chicken stock
50ml double cream

To garnish ...
100g mixed mushrooms
2 teaspoons fresh parsley, chopped
1 tablespoon olive oil
squeeze of lemon juice
truffle oil, to taste
Heart-shaped croutons

- Soak the porcini mushrooms in 150ml of boiling water for 30 minutes, then strain to remove any grit and reserve the liquor. Roughly chop and set to one side.
- Meanwhile, heat the butter and oil in a frying pan, add the shallots and garlic, then sweat until softened. Add the 250g mixed mushrooms and thyme and fry until browned.
- Transfer to a saucepan, then add the porcini mushrooms, reserved liquor and stock. Bring to the boil, then cover and simmer gently for 15–20 minutes.
- Meanwhile, reheat the frying pan to create the garnish. Add the olive oil and mixed mushrooms to the pan, then fry quickly until brown. Season to taste, then add the lemon juice and parsley.
- Blend the soup in the saucepan until completely smooth, and gently add the cream while reheating.
- Divide the soup into bowls, garnish with the mushrooms, then serve with heart-shaped croutons and a good drizzle of truffle oil.

Spice Up Your Night
King Prawn, Chilli & Ginger

This soup looks and tastes fantastic but is surprisingly easy to make. Even the most culinarily challenged can manage it, so chaps, there's no excuse for not producing a romantic meal for the love of your life.

With spicy chilli and ginger this will set the taste buds tingling, and the rich colours will add warmth to the occasion. Everything works in this recipe to impress and delight the one you love.

Serves 2

Cooking time: 10 minutes

14 raw king prawns
1 stick lemongrass
250ml fish stock
1 x 200ml tin coconut milk
1cm piece ginger, grated
1 teaspoon sugar
1 tablespoon lime juice
1 tablespoon fish sauce
1 red chilli, finely sliced
half tablespoon red Thai curry paste
5g fresh coriander leaves, shredded
few springs fresh mint, shredded

- Remove the tough outer layer of the lemongrass, bash with a knife to bruise and release the flavour, then cut in half.
- Place the lemongrass, curry paste, hot stock, chilli, ginger and coconut milk in a saucepan and simmer gently for 5 minutes.
- Add the king prawns, fish sauce, lime and sugar, then simmer for a further 3 minutes until the prawns are cooked.
- Remove the lemongrass pieces and serve topped with the mint and coriander.

Cupid's Arrow
Asparagus Spears with Parma Ham

State your intentions with a soup that'll go straight to your valentine's heart. Cupid will certainly be around to help when you make this deliciously creamy creation. Whether or not you believe that asparagus is an aphrodisiac, this soup will certainly set the mood for a *diner à deux*.

You can spell out your love and get your message across by creative use of the asparagus spears and Parma ham. We hope you both enjoy the evening.

Cooking time: 25 minutes

Serves 2

250g asparagus
25g butter
350ml chicken stock
25ml single cream
half celery stick, sliced
1 leek, sliced
half tablespoon plain flour
2 slices Parma ham

- Cut the tips of the asparagus to about 6cm in length and set to one side.
- Chop the asparagus stalks into 2–3cm lengths, discarding the tough ends.
- Melt the butter in a saucepan, add the leeks and celery, then cover and sweat, without browning, for 10–15 minutes until softened.
- Add the flour, stir, then cook for a minute or so. Add the asparagus stalks and stock.
- Cover and simmer for 5–7 minutes until the asparagus is just tender but still has its colour and bite.
- Meanwhile, heat the grill, season the asparagus, then drizzle over a little olive oil.
- Place the asparagus spears and Parma ham slices under the grill until the asparagus is slightly charred and the Parma ham is crispy.
- Blend the soup until completely smooth, then add the cream while gently reheating. Season to taste.
- Pour the soup into bowls and place the asparagus spears and Parma ham on top.

Fennel Soup with Lobster

This inspired combination comes from a bit of lateral thinking by Owen Evans, one of our top Soup of the Month creators. Owen is a real romantic, who regularly enjoys spoiling his girlfriend, Susie, by taking her out for dinner.

After a visit to one of the lucky girl's most loved seafood restaurants, he was prompted to create this spectacular recipe. It has become one of Susie's favourites. So if it works for Owen, it could be well worth you giving it a try.

Serves 4

Cooking time: 1 hour

150g lobster flesh
2 tablespoons olive oil
2 shallots, sliced
1 stick celery, chopped
3 fennel bulbs, sliced
700ml fish stock
1 bay leaf
100ml dry white wine
100ml double cream
1 tablespoon fresh parsley, chopped

- Heat the oil in a saucepan, add the celery, shallots and fennel, then cook for 10 minutes until softened.
- Add the wine and simmer to reduce by half.
- Add the stock and bayleaf and bring to the boil. Cover and simmer for 30–40 minutes until the fennel is tender.
- Remove the bay leaf and blend. Pass through a sieve, using the back of a ladle to push it through.
- Reheat gently, add the cream and season to taste.
- Serve the soup topped with a sprinkle of parsley and the lobster flesh.

Love & Hearts
Artichoke Hearts with Parmesan Croutons

The dedicated romantic will slave over fresh artichokes to have everything right for their loved one, but we reckon that tinned ones will do the job just as well for this luxurious creamy treat. Whichever you choose, you can be sure this soup won't let you down.

You can always make up for your lack of artichoke-peeling with heart-shaped bowls and a candle-lit table scattered with rose petals.

Cooking time: 30 minutes

Serves 2

For the soup ...
- 25g butter
- 1 x 240g tin globe artichoke hearts, cut into chunks
- 2 teaspoons fresh thyme, chopped
- 1 bay leaf
- 350ml chicken stock
- 75ml single cream
- 1 small onion, chopped
- 2 teaspoons chives, snipped

For the croutons ...
- ciabatta bread, sliced at an angle
- 1 clove garlic
- 25g parmesan, grated

- Melt the butter in a saucepan, add the onion and cook for 5 minutes.
- Add the artichokes, thyme and bay leaf, then sweat for a further 5 minutes until tender but without browning.
- Add the stock, then cover and simmer for 10-15 minutes until really tender.
- Remove the bay leaf and puree until very smooth. Reheat gently, add the cream and season to taste.
- To make the croutons ... toast each slice of ciabatta, then rub with the garlic clove.
- Serve the soup with a scattering of chives, a floating crouton with parmesan sprinkled over the top and a drizzle of olive oil.

Lovers' Dish
Mussel, Tomato & Basil

What is it about Italians? They have a wonderful way with food and are reputed to be the best lovers in Europe. This tasty delight is designed to be shared by two eating from a single platter as you gaze into each other's eyes.

While you eat, imagine the splendour of Venice and the romance of the gondolier's song. Savour the moment as well as the soup, and you'll find this is one dish that could take longer to eat than it does to cook.

Serves 2

Cooking time: 25 minutes

1kg mussels, cleaned and de-bearded
5 shallots, finely sliced
2 cloves garlic, finely sliced
4 tablespoons olive oil
500g plum tomatoes, peeled, de-seeded and chopped
small bunch fresh basil
150ml dry white wine
focaccia bread to serve

- Heat 2 tablespoons of olive oil in a saucepan, fry the shallots and half of the garlic until lightly browned.
- Add the tomatoes and half the basil leaves, then cook over a medium to high heat until they reduce to a thick sauce (around 15 minutes).
- Heat the remaining olive oil in a large pan, fry the rest of the garlic briefly and toss the mussels into the oil. Pour in the white wine, then cover and cook over a high heat until the mussels have opened.
- Tip the mussels into a colander with a bowl underneath to reserve the juices, then quickly remove at least half of the mussels from their shells.
- Add all the mussels to the sauce, add the reserved cooking liquor and reheat well.
- Add the remaining basil, season well and serve with a drizzle of extra virgin olive oil and warm focaccia bread.

Sausage & Stout

This is a great family favourite of Mike Tucknott, who tells us which soups to make and when. It packs warming flavours into an easily made soup. His wife, Cate, makes sure that he doesn't forget the sausages while his mind is on the beer.

When the Tucknott family are heading off to the local fireworks display, they feast on this first. To make sure there are no unfilled corners of the family tummies, they ladle the soup into nice big Yorkshire puddings.

Serves 4

Cooking time: 50 minutes

16 cocktail sausages
3 medium onions, finely sliced
500ml beef stock
300ml dark stout
2 tablespoons plain flour
2 tablespoons olive oil
1 tablespoon fresh thyme, finely chopped
1 tablespoon fresh parsley, finely chopped
2 small carrots, diced small
1 medium potato, diced small
2 teaspoons Dijon mustard
2 teaspoons Worcestershire sauce
1 tablespoon redcurrant jelly

- Fry the sausages for 8–10 minutes until browned, then set to one side.
- In the same pan, heat the oil and fry the onions until well browned. Add the flour and stout, stirring continuously until you have a thick sauce.
- Transfer to a saucepan, then add the stock and thyme. Bring to a simmer and add the sauces.
- Cover and simmer for 15 minutes.
- Meanwhile, in a separate pan, simmer the carrots and potato until almost cooked through.
- Strain the carrots and potato, then add these to the stock pan, along with the mustard, Worcestershire sauce and redcurrant jelly. Simmer for a further 5 minutes, season to taste and serve with crusty bread.

Bangers & Creamy Mash

When you're expecting hungry hordes in your garden for your fireworks and bonfire party, this hearty soup will keep everyone happy. It's good, honest food, which enables you to smuggle potatoes and cabbage past the children.

We find the children enjoy arranging the sausages into interesting shapes – and since they're outside in the dark, granny can't object to them playing with their food.

Serves 4

Cooking time: 35 minutes

500g floury potatoes, diced
24 cocktail sausages
50g butter
1 onion, diced
600ml chicken stock
100g cream cheese
200g savoy cabbage, cored and finely shredded
4 tablespoons fresh pesto

- Melt half the butter in a saucepan, add the onion and potatoes, then cover and sweat without browning for 10 minutes.
- Add the stock and simmer for a further 20 minutes until the potatoes are soft.
- Meanwhile, heat the remaining butter in a saucepan, add the cabbage and 2 tablespoons of water to the pan, cover and cook until just tender. Season to taste.
- Fry the sausages until cooked and golden brown.
- Add the cream cheese to the soup, then puree.
- Reheat the soup, adjust the seasoning and serve topped with the cabbage, sausages and a drizzle of pesto.

Pumpkin with Crispy Chorizo

Although Halloween is always looked on as a night for the children, there's no reason why adults shouldn't enjoy themselves too. This is a grown-up soup devised by Lez Down, who not only ensures we make our soup well but is also a keen grower of pumpkins. However, his plan to provide different food for the adults and children to eat never works – because the children love this too.

They particularly enjoy their own version of apple bobbing with this recipe – trying to get their teeth into the floating slices of chorizo straight from the colourful and spicy soup. Great fun, but try to avoid burnt noses.

Serves 4

Cooking time: 40 minutes

650g pumpkin flesh
25g butter
1 tablespoon olive oil
2–3 fresh sage leaves
1 red chilli, de-seeded and chopped
650ml chicken stock
1 medium onion, diced
2 cloves garlic, diced
100g chorizo, diced

- Heat the oil and butter in a saucepan, add the onion, chilli and sage, then cook for 10 minutes until well softened.
- Add the pumpkin flesh and sweat for a couple of minutes. Pour in the stock, then cover and simmer for 20–25 minutes.
- Meanwhile, fry the chorizo and garlic until the chorizo is browned and the garlic crispy.
- Blend the soup, season to taste, then reheat gently, adding the chorizo and garlic, along with the chorizo oil.

Witches' Brew
Pumpkin Soup

If you've ever wondered how to get something more nourishing than sugary treats into your little witches and wizards, this works every time. They'll find it very comforting food for what can be a scary evening.

The vibrant colours served in a hollowed-out pumpkin are a brilliant way to get little people eating good food. When they're well fed and warm inside they'll be ready for the fun.

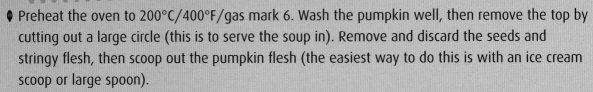

Serves 8–10

Cooking time: 40 minutes

1 medium to large pumpkin (1.2kg flesh or 4kg whole)
3 tablespoons olive oil
2 medium onions, chopped
1 teaspoon ground cinnamon
2 bay leaves
2 cloves garlic
1.3 litres chicken stock
4 tablespoons single cream
1 teaspoon ground cumin
3 tablespoons fresh pesto, mixed with olive to drizzle over the soup

Witches' broomsticks: 1 ready rolled puff pastry sheet
1 egg
grated parmesan

- Preheat the oven to 200°C/400°F/gas mark 6. Wash the pumpkin well, then remove the top by cutting out a large circle (this is to serve the soup in). Remove and discard the seeds and stringy flesh, then scoop out the pumpkin flesh (the easiest way to do this is with an ice cream scoop or large spoon).
- Heat the oil in a saucepan and fry the onions and garlic for 10 minutes until softened.
- Add the pumpkin flesh, spices and bay leaves, then cook for a further 5 minutes.
- Add the stock, bring to the boil, then cover and simmer for 20 minutes until the pumpkin is tender.
- Meanwhile, cut witches' broomstick shapes out of the puff pastry sheets, place on a baking tray and brush with beaten egg. Sprinkle with parmesan and bake for 15 minutes.
- When the pumpkin is tender, remove the bay leaves from the soup and blend until smooth.
- Reheat gently, adding the cream, then season to taste.
- Pour into the hollowed-out pumpkin and serve with a drizzle of pesto and witches' broomsticks.

Smoked Chicken Chowder

Our Per Hogberg confesses that one of his favourite smells is the 'delicate' aroma of the smoke in the air. As a confirmed bonfire enthusiast, he comes into his own on 5th November. When he has built and lit his annual creation, he likes nothing better than the smoky chicken soup he devised to suit the occasion.

As a chunky soup, it's packed with all sorts of good things. If you're going to pour it into a flask, a quick blitz in the food processor will give a smooth soup to sip around the bonfire.

Serves 4

Cooking time: 40 minutes

100g cooked smoked chicken, diced
100g smoked streaky bacon, diced
1 tablespoon olive oil
1 small onion, diced
1 stick celery, chopped
1 large potato, diced
800ml water
100g sweetcorn, fresh or frozen
100ml single cream
1 tablespoon fresh parsley, chopped

- Fry the bacon until crispy and golden, then drain on kitchen paper and set aside.
- Heat the oil in a saucepan and sweat the onion and celery for 5–10 minutes until softened, without browning.
- Add the potato and water, bring to the boil, then cover and simmer for 10–15 minutes until the potato is almost tender.
- Add the sweetcorn and cook for a further 5–7 minutes.
- Add the cream, smoked chicken and bacon, then heat and stir until thoroughly warmed through.
- Season to taste with pepper only (the chicken and bacon are salty enough), then sprinkle with parsley and serve.
- For a smoother soup to put in your flask, simply add a little milk when blending.

Slow Roasted Tomato & Basil

You can't go wrong with tomato soup when you're feeding all ages and tastes on a special outdoor occasion like bonfire night. Our chefs were inspired by roaring fires to create a colourful soup that's perfect for standing around outside.

Slow roasting gives the tomatoes a wonderful depth of flavour that tantalises the tastebuds and reaches right down to the toes.

Serves 4

Cooking time: 1 hour 10 minutes

1kg ripe tomatoes, halved
1 red onion, cut into 6 wedges
2 cloves garlic, unpeeled
1 red pepper, de-seeded then cut into large strips
2 tablespoons olive oil
2 tablespoons balsamic vinegar
1 teaspoon caster sugar
10g fresh basil leaves, chopped
400ml vegetable stock

- Preheat your oven to 170°C/325°F/gas mark 3.
- Arrange the tomatoes, cut side facing up, in roasting tins, then place the red pepper, onion and garlic cloves around the tomatoes. Drizzle with olive oil and balsamic vinegar and season well with salt and pepper.
- Sprinkle the sugar over the top and roast for 1 hour. The tomatoes should have dried out a little and the pepper and onion should be soft.
- Peel the roasted garlic, then blend the roasted tomatoes, roasted vegetables, stock and basil until fairly smooth.
- Pour into a saucepan, reheat, season to taste and serve.

Little Black Dress Soup
Hot & Sour Chicken

The girls in our office call this their Little Black Dress soup because it fits brilliantly with one of their Christmas worries. It's so light that it's virtually a salad in a bowl, so it doesn't threaten their hips in the all important couple of weeks before the party season.

With ginger, lemongrass and chilli, it's a tasty way to detox, so they're often still relying on this well into the New Year.

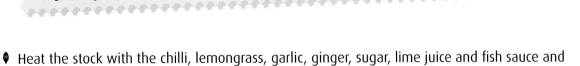

Cooking time: 15 minutes

Serves 4

2 chicken breasts
1 litre chicken stock
2–3 red chillies, de-seeded and finely sliced
1 stick lemongrass, inner part only, finely sliced
1 clove garlic, finely sliced
2cm piece ginger, cut into fine strips
4 spring onions, finely sliced
20g fresh coriander, chopped
1 teaspoon sugar
1 lime, juice of
3 tablespoons fish sauce
150g baby chestnut mushrooms, quartered

- Heat the stock with the chilli, lemongrass, garlic, ginger, sugar, lime juice and fish sauce and bring to the boil.
- Add the mushrooms and simmer for 3–4 minutes.
- Meanwhile, place the chicken breasts in a sheet of cling film and beat with a rolling pin until thin (like an escalope). Season the chicken before dry frying it for 3–4 minutes on each side until cooked through.
- Slice the cooked chicken thinly, then place piles into each of the serving bowls, alongside the spring onions and coriander.
- Pour the soup over the top of the chicken, spring onions and coriander, then serve.

Christmas Wrapping
Turkey & all the Trimmings

When you're tired of sandwiches and curry, you'll be looking for a new way to make the most of the inevitable leftovers. With this mouth-watering soup, you can use most of them, including the stock from the carcass, so you get all the flavours of the traditional dinner.

While you know you are clearing out the fridge, it won't taste like it. This is a delicious dish in its own right, although you may find that floating the trimmings on top gives the game away a little.

Serves 4

Cooking time: 45 minutes

850ml turkey stock
100g turkey meat
2 small carrots, diced
half small swede, diced
2 small parsnips, diced
1 small onion, diced
1 tablespoon fresh thyme, chopped
2 tablespoons olive oil
1 tablespoon fresh parsley, chopped

trimmings ...   8 stuffing balls
8 cocktail sausages
8 rolled-up rashers of bacon

- Heat the oil in a saucepan, then sweat all the vegetables for 10 minutes without browning.
- Add the thyme and stock, then cover and simmer for 20 minutes.
- Add the turkey and cook for a further 10 minutes.
- Meanwhile, reheat the stuffing balls, sausages and rolled-up bacon rashers until they are piping hot.
- Blend the soup, then reheat gently, adding the parsley and seasoning to taste.
- Pour the soup into bowls and serve with the trimmings on top.

Parsnip in a Pear Tree
Spicy Parsnip & Pear

This intriguing combination of flavours is a worthy gift for your true love on the first day of Christmas. Parsnips are easier to find than partridges and the traditional gift would get you into trouble if your true love were vegetarian.

The distinctive seasonal taste of parsnip is offset by the fruity tang of pear, giving a lovely creamy soup, which is the ideal way to start off a Christmas feast.

Cooking time: 40 minutes

Serves 4

800ml vegetable stock
3 large (500g) parsnips, chopped
100ml single cream
1 medium onion, diced
1 pear, peeled and diced
3 tablespoons olive oil
1 clove garlic, crushed
1cm piece ginger, chopped
1 teaspoon garam masala
1 teaspoon ground cumin
1 teaspoon ground coriander

- Heat the oil in a saucepan, then add the onion and garlic and cook until softened.
- Add the garam masala, cumin, coriander and ginger, then stir well and fry for 1–2 minutes.
- Add the parsnips and stock, then bring to the boil, cover and simmer for 30 minutes until the vegetables are tender.
- Add the pear and blend until smooth.
- Reheat gently, adding the cream and stirring well.
- Serve with vegetable crisps as a garnish (see page 116).

Chestnuts Roasting on an Open Fire
Mushroom & Roasted Chestnut

For us the smell of roasting chestnuts tells us that Christmas is on the way. It conjures up Dickensian scenes of street sellers, carol singers and roaring log fires.

So this traditional image was in our minds when we came up with this soup as a great way to set the scene for your Christmas celebrations. The chestnut aroma mingles with the earthy flavour of mushrooms to give an old-fashioned taste of winter.

Serves 4

Cooking time: 35 minutes

400g mixed mushrooms, sliced (we use portabello, girolle, shiitake and chestnut)
150g ready-roasted chestnuts, sliced
3 tablespoons olive oil
1 stick celery, chopped
1 small carrot, diced
1 small onion, diced
1 tablespoon fresh parsley, chopped
1 tablespoon soy sauce
1 bay leaf

- Add the stock, celery, onion, carrot and bay leaf to a pan, then bring to the boil, cover and simmer for 20 minutes.
- Meanwhile, heat the oil in a frying pan and fry the mushrooms until browned. Add the chestnuts, then fry for a couple more minutes. Set 6 tablespoons of the chestnut and mushroom mix to one side for garnishing.
- Add the fried mushrooms and remaining chestnuts to the stock saucepan, then simmer for a further 10 minutes.
- Remove the bay leaf and blend until smooth. Reheat gently, adding the soy sauce.
- Put a spoonful of the set-aside mushrooms and chestnuts in each serving bowl, then pour the soup on top, sprinkle with parsley and serve.

White Christmas
White Onion, Stilton & Sherry

Even if your dreams of falling snow flakes and a magical white covering don't come true, you can create your own white magic in a bowl for Christmas Eve.

With these festive flavours and a hint of seasonal booze, this recipe will get you in the mood to snuggle up in front of the fire and listen to all your traditional Christmas songs. It's so Christmassy, you may even find yourself singing along with Bing Crosby as you make it.

Cooking time: 45 minutes

Serves 4

600ml vegetable stock
1 large potato, diced
1 small onion, diced
2 tablespoons olive oil
2 tablespoons flour
100g Stilton cheese, diced
2 tablespoons sweet sherry (or dessert wine)
1 medium onion, sliced
1 tablespoon fresh parsley, finely chopped
1 tablespoon fresh thyme, finely chopped
150ml milk
50 ml double cream

- Heat half the olive oil in a frying pan, then fry the sliced onions for 10 minutes until they are soft and translucent. Remove from the pan and set aside.
- Heat the rest of the oil in a saucepan, add the diced onions and fry until translucent.
- Add the potato, stock and thyme to the saucepan, bring to the boil, then cover and simmer for 10–15 minutes until the vegetables are tender.
- Remove from the heat and stir in the Stilton cheese until melted. Blend until completely smooth.
- Mix the flour with a little water, stir to form a paste, then add to the saucepan, along with the fried sliced onions, sherry and milk.
- Reheat gently for a further 5–10 minutes, stirring to thicken the soup and warm through the onions.
- Stir in the double cream, season to taste and serve sprinkled with parsley.

Gold, Frankincense & Myrrh
Golden Saffron Soup

Of course everyone at NCG is soup mad, but often the enthusiasm extends to their families too. Hannah, wife of our Colin Wilson, heard that we were looking for seasonal recipes and came bearing this delightful gift.

It's a hearty soup packed with goodness that'll give a warm feeling inside to go with the golden glow from the saffron. Truly fit for kings.

Serves 4

Cooking time: 40 minutes

Good pinch saffron strands
3 medium onions, finely chopped (reserve the skins)
3 medium potatoes, peeled and chopped
1 clove garlic, chopped
25g butter
1 tablespoon olive oil
650ml chicken stock
150ml single cream
1 tablespoon lemon juice

- Soak the saffron strands in 50ml boiling water and set aside.
- Wash the brown onion skins (they will add flavour and colour to the soup).
- Heat the butter and oil in a saucepan, add the onions and onion skins, then sweat for 10 minutes.
- Add the potato and garlic and cook for a further 5–10 minutes so that the onions take on a golden colour.
- Add the stock and soaked saffron, then cover and simmer for 15 minutes until the potatoes are cooked.
- Remove the onion skins and discard, then blend the soup.
- Reheat the blended soup gently, stir in the cream, season to taste and add the lemon juice to taste before serving.

Celeriac & Bacon

An epic Boxing Day mountain bike ride has become a tradition for Nikki Churchill, our creative wordsmith, and hubby Mark. During their seasonal travels visiting friends and family back home in the South West, festive indulgencies hit them at every stop.

So whilst Mark loads their bikes onto the car, Nikki works up this wonderful, winter warmer destined for flasks in their backpacks, then they set off keen and determined to conquer the Quantock Hills before they themselves are conquered by the extra Christmas calories.

Cooking time: 35 minutes

Serves 4

300g celeriac, diced
10 rashers streaky bacon
1 medium leek, diced
750ml water
25g butter
1 bay leaf
50ml double cream
1 large potato, diced
squeeze fresh lemon juice

- Roughly chop approximately half the bacon rashers. Heat the butter in a saucepan, then add the chopped bacon and leeks and cook until softened.
- Add the celeriac, potato, stock, lemon juice and bay leaf, then bring to the boil. Simmer for 20–25 minutes until the vegetables are tender.
- Meanwhile, fry the remaining bacon rashers until crispy. Drain on kitchen paper and set aside for garnishing.
- Remove the bay leaf, then blend the soup until smooth, reheat gently and add the cream.
- Serve with the crispy bacon rashers crumbled on top of the soup.

Wilted Spinach & Stilton

One of the most predictable parts of Christmas for Sally Beckett, our recipe queen, is the gift of a Stilton for her cheese board from her great uncle. There's got to be a limit to the amount of cheese and crackers that a girl can eat, so Sally has become adept at finding novel ways to use up some of the extra.

Here she combines the vibrant colour of spinach with the tanginess of her great uncle's gift to make an unusual soup that works brilliantly on the tastebuds of friends gathered to compare gifts at a post-Christmas supper.

Serves 4

Cooking time: 35 minutes

100g Stilton cheese, crumbled
700ml vegetable stock
50g crème fraîche
50g butter
2 leeks, sliced
500g spinach leaves
1 medium potato, diced

- Melt the butter in a saucepan, then sweat the leeks for 5 minutes until softened.
- Add the potato, cook for 2–3 minutes and add the stock.
- Bring to the boil, cover and simmer gently for 15–20 minutes until the potato is tender.
- Meanwhile, wash the spinach really well and drain. Place in a separate saucepan of boiling water and stir over a medium heat until just wilted. Drain.
- Stir the crumbled Stilton into the potato/leek saucepan until melted. Add the drained spinach, then blend.
- Reheat gently, then stir in the crème fraîche. Season to taste and serve.

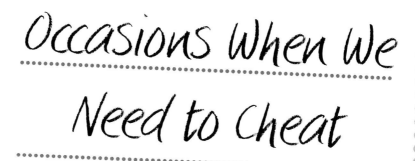

Occasions When We Need to Cheat

Quick & Easy Soups   Cheating With Our Soups

For those occasions when we need to cheat

Shortcuts to soup

As you're a soup lover, you're usually happy to spend a while putting together your creations so that you and your family can enjoy the great variety of freshly made soup. However, let's be honest. There are times when you are a bit pushed and a shortcut would really help.

So we asked our chefs to rack their brains (and swallow a bit of professional pride) and give you some hints on how to prepare a tasty soup when you also have to attend to homework, catch up on emails or just want to relax and read a magazine.

Some of these recipes use ready-mixed ingredients you'll find on any supermarket shelf. Some suggest a trip to the freezer aisle to save on chopping and cooking time. Either way, you'll end up with a great tasting soup. And if you don't leave the book open at this page, no-one else need ever know.

The ultimate fresh ingredient

Our fresh soup is goodness in a carton and acts as a great base for a fresh and nutritious meal. So this chapter will also provide you with some tasty shortcuts to feeding the family or cooking up a quick lunch for friends using our soups.

Whether you're making a risotto, a pie or a casserole, you can rely on all the efforts we make to give you a great tasting meal. Just a carton of our fresh soup will transform other fresh produce, store-cupboard ingredients or leftovers into a satisfying dish.

When you have tried these recipes, you'll probably have your own idea of variations that you could use. Enjoy experimenting.

Chicken Miso Broth

Serves 4
Cooking time: 10 minutes

2 sachets instant miso soup
400ml chicken stock (from
concentrate or cube)
150g pack cooked medium egg or
udon noodles
150g pak choi, roughly chopped
150g cooked chicken breast, sliced
2 teaspoons Thai fish sauce
4 spring onions, finely sliced into
strips

- Place stock, miso sachet contents, 500ml boiling water and fish sauce in a large saucepan, bring to the boil, then reduce to a simmer.
- Add the chicken and pak choi and cook for 2–3 minutes.
- Stir in the noodles and cook for a further minute or so to heat the noodles.
- Serve in large flat bowls, sprinkled with spring onion and soy sauce to taste.

Plum Tomato & Basil

Serves 4
Cooking time: 30 minutes

80g tomato puree
2 teaspoons caster sugar
2 tablespoons olive oil
1 teaspoon basil puree
500g passata with onion & garlic
400ml water
1 x 400g tin chopped plum
tomatoes with garlic & herbs
1 tablespoon fresh basil, chopped

- Place all the ingredients in a saucepan, stir well and bring to the boil.
- Cover and simmer for 20 minutes.
- Season to taste, then stir through the fresh basil and serve.

Watercress, Soya Bean & Pesto

Serves 4
Cooking time: 10 minutes

1 tablespoon olive oil
8 spring onions, sliced
200g watercress
1 teaspoon garlic puree
300g frozen soya beans
800ml chicken stock
3 tablespoons fresh pesto
2 teaspoons lemon juice

- Heat the oil in a saucepan, add the spring onions and garlic, then fry for 3 minutes.
- Add the stock and soya beans, bring back to the boil and cook for 2 minutes.
- Add the watercress, then cook for a further 3 minutes.
- Blend until smooth.
- Add the lemon juice and pesto and stir through.
- Season to taste and serve.

Tuscan Bean

Serves 4
Cooking time: 25 minutes

1 x 400g tin mixed beans
600ml vegetable stock (from concentrate or cube)
110g pancetta, cubed
1 teaspoon dried mixed herbs
pinch of chilli powder
1 x 400g tin chopped tomatoes with onion & basil
1 teaspoon garlic puree

- Fry the pancetta in a frying pan until golden brown, then drain on kitchen paper.
- Meanwhile, place all the other ingredients into a saucepan, bring to the boil, then cover and simmer for 10 minutes.
- Add the pancetta to the saucepan, then cover and simmer for a further 10 minutes.
- Season to taste and serve.

Pea & Ham

Serves 4
Cooking time: 15 minutes

500g frozen peas
500ml ham stock (from cube)
150g Wiltshire cured sliced ham,
diced
5 spring onions, sliced
100ml milk
25g butter

- Heat the butter in a saucepan and fry the spring onions for 2–3 minutes.
- Add the hot stock, bring to the boil, then add the peas.
- Keep on a high heat and quickly bring back to the boil. Once boiling, add the ham before reducing the heat and simmering for 5 minutes.
- Blend until smooth, add the milk, then reheat gently.
- Season to taste and serve.

Butternut Squash & Goats' Cheese

Serves 4
Cooking time: 35 minutes

2 tablespoons olive oil
150g frozen diced onion
1 teaspoon dried sage
800g frozen, cubed butternut
squash
1 teaspoon garlic puree
600ml vegetable stock (from
concentrate or cube)
100g soft, mild goats' cheese,
crumbled

- Heat the oil in a large saucepan and fry the onion until soft.
- Add the garlic, sage and butternut squash, then cook over a medium heat for 5–10 minutes, stirring occasionally.
- Add the stock, bring back to the boil, then cover and simmer for 10 minutes or until the squash is tender.
- Stir in the goats' cheese until melted.
- Blend until smooth, reheat gently, then season to taste and serve.

Chicken, Leek & Parmesan Tart

Serves 4–6
Cooking time: 35–40 minutes

300g (half carton) NCG Chicken Soup
1 x large (230g) fresh shortcrust pastry case
2 small leeks, thinly sliced
25g butter
2 eggs
25g grated parmesan
60g cooked chicken breast, thinly sliced

- Preheat a baking tray in the oven 200°C/400°F/ gas mark 6.
- Melt the butter in a frying pan, cook the leeks for a few minutes until soft, then allow to cool.
- Place the leeks in the bottom of the pastry case, then top with the chicken.
- Mix the eggs, NCG chicken soup, some black pepper and half the parmesan together, then pour into the pastry case.
- Sprinkle over the remaining parmesan and place the foil-lined pastry case onto the pre-heated baking tray.
- Bake for 30 minutes or so until golden brown and set.

Fish Pie

Serves 6
Cooking time: 1 hour

900g seafood medley or fish pie mix (fresh or defrosted from frozen)
3 eggs
1 x 600g carton NCG Smoked Haddock Chowder
900g frozen mashed potato discs
2 tablespoons chives, chopped
150g grated mature cheddar cheese
1 glass white wine
2 tablespoons plain flour

- Preheat oven 200°C/400°F/ gas mark 6.
- Hard boil the eggs, allow to cool, and cut into chunks.
- Place the fish in a wide saucepan, add the wine, then bring to a gentle simmer, cover and cook for 5 minutes.
- Transfer the fish to an ovenproof dish.
- Put the saucepan back onto the heat and reduce the cooking liquor until you have 3 tablespoons. Add the soup and bring to a gentle simmer.
- Mix the flour with a little water and add to the soup mix. Stir and simmer for 3 minutes until thickened.
- Meanwhile, defrost the mash according to pack instructions and add most of the cheese, leaving a little for the top.
- Add the eggs, chives and sauce to the fish pie dish, top with mashed potato and cheese and bake for 30–40 minutes until piping hot and golden.

Chilli Tacos

Serves 4
Cooking time: 25 minutes

500g beef mince
1 x 420g tin red kidney beans in chilli sauce
1 teaspoon garlic puree
1 x 600g carton NCG Plum Tomato & Basil soup
1 tablespoon olive oil
1 teaspoon ground cinnamon
1 teaspoon ground cumin
1 teaspoon ground coriander
1 teaspoon chilli puree (optional)
1 medium onion, diced
8–12 taco shells
half lettuce, shredded
200g grated cheese
Tex Mex dip selection

- Heat the oil in a saucepan and fry the onion, garlic and spices for a few minutes until the onion is soft and spices aromatic.
- Add the mince and fry until browned, then add the soup and kidney beans in their sauce. Bring to the boil and simmer for 20 minutes.
- Warm the taco shells, then serve the chilli in a large bowl with small bowls of lettuce, cheese and dips.

This also tastes great with tortillas.

Bolognese

Serves 4
Cooking time: 35–40 minutes

500g beef mince
110g cubed pancetta
1 teaspoon garlic puree
1 x 600g carton NCG Plum Tomato & Basil soup
1 teaspoon dried oregano
100ml red wine (optional)
10g fresh basil leaves, torn
25g grated parmesan

- Heat a large saucepan and fry the pancetta and mince until browned.
- Drain off any excess fat, then add the garlic puree, oregano and red wine. Simmer until almost all the liquid has evaporated.
- Add the soup, stir well, then simmer for a further 20 minutes.
- Stir in the fresh basil, season to taste and serve topped with parmesan.

Spicy Spaghetti Bake

Serves 4 generously

Cooking time: 1 hour

500g beef mince
150g frozen diced onion
1 teaspoon garlic puree
2 tablespoons basil oil
1 x 600g NCG Plum Tomato &
Mascarpone Soup
1 x 400g tin chopped tomatoes with
basil and oregano
2 teaspoons garam masala
pinch of chilli powder
150g grated mature cheddar cheese
150g sliced frozen mushrooms
280g spaghetti or linguine

- Preheat the oven to 180°C/350°F/ gas mark 4.
- Heat the oil in a saucepan, then fry the mushrooms and onions until softened, draining off any excess liquid.
- Add the mince and brown for a few minutes. Add the spices and cook for a minute or two before adding the soup and tomatoes.
- Bring to the boil, then simmer for 20 minutes.
- Meanwhile, cook the spaghetti until *al-dente*.
- Drain the spaghetti, stir in the meat sauce and pour into an ovenproof dish.
- Sprinkle with cheese and bake for 30 minutes until the cheese is brown and bubbling.

Chicken, Mushroom & Bacon Lasagne

Serves 4–6

Cooking time: 45 minutes

6 rashers smoked streaky bacon,
roughly sliced
250g chestnut mushrooms, sliced
500g pack chicken breasts, diced
1 x 600g carton NCG Chicken Soup
1 x 350g tub cheese sauce
1 tablespoon plain flour
4 tablespoons grated parmesan
9 (approximately) lasagne sheets
4 tablespoons fresh breadcrumbs
1 tablespoon wholegrain mustard

- Preheat the oven to 190°C/375°F/ gas mark 5.
- Fry the bacon in a saucepan until golden, then add the mushrooms and stir.
- Toss the chicken in the flour until coated well, before adding to the saucepan with any remaining flour.
- Cook the chicken until golden and the mushrooms are cooked, adding a little olive oil if necessary.
- Pour in the soup and add the mustard, bring to a simmer for 2 minutes, stirring continuously.
- In a large ovenproof dish, layer the chicken filling and lasagne sheets three times, finishing with a layer of lasagne on top.
- Pour over the cheese sauce, then sprinkle over the breadcrumbs and parmesan.
- Bake for 35–45 minutes until golden.

Sweet Potato & Spinach Dhal

Serves 4
Cooking time: 45 minutes

100g red lentils
100g green lentils
350g sweet potato cubes, fresh or frozen
1 x 400g tin ready-fried onions
1 x 250g bag spinach leaves
1 x 600g carton NCG Spicy Butternut Squash & Sweet Potato Soup
1 teaspoon ginger puree
1 teaspoon garlic puree
2 teaspoons garam masala

- Rinse the lentils and place in a saucepan of cold water. Bring to the boil, then boil rapidly for 10 minutes.
- Rinse, then drain.
- Using the same saucepan, add the fried onions, garlic, ginger and garam masala and fry for 2–3 minutes until fragrant.
- Add the lentils and soup, then cover and simmer for 15 minutes.
- Add the sweet potato cubes, stir and cook for a further 10 minutes.
- Add the spinach leaves, stir, then leave for a few minutes to wilt.
- Season to taste and serve with pilau rice, naan bread and a dollop of natural yogurt.

Gnocchi with Grilled Vegetables & Gorgonzola

Serves 4
Cooking time: 15 minutes

500g frozen grilled vegetables
1 tablespoon basil oil
1 x 600g carton NCG Plum Tomato & Mascarpone Soup
2 handfuls fresh breadcrumbs
50g grated parmesan
100g Gorgonzola cheese, diced
500g fresh gnocchi

- Heat the basil oil in a saucepan, then fry the grilled vegetables for 4–6 minutes until hot.
- Add the soup and heat through.
- Meanwhile, cook the gnocchi in a saucepan of boiling water for 2 minutes or until they float. Drain, then add to the tomato and vegetable sauce.
- Stir gently before pouring into an ovenproof dish. Scatter the Gorgonzola cubes, breadcrumbs and parmesan over the top, then grill for 3–5 minutes until golden and bubbling.
- Serve with a large mixed-leaf salad.

To make ahead, simply follow the recipe above but do not grill. Cool then refrigerate.
When ready to eat, simply bake in a pre-heated oven for 30 minutes (190°C/375°F/gas mark 5).

Wild Mushroom & Spinach Risotto

Serves 3–4
Cooking time: 35–40 minutes

1 large onion, diced
50g butter
300ml vegetable stock (from concentrate or cube)
300g risotto rice
250g chestnut mushrooms, sliced
1 x 600g carton NCG Wild Mushroom Soup
100g grated parmesan
100g spinach leaves
250ml white wine

- Melt the butter in a saucepan, then fry the onions until soft. Stir in the mushrooms and cook for 5 minutes.
- Add the rice and wine, then cook and stir until most of the wine is absorbed. Add the soup and bring to a gentle simmer, stirring frequently.
- Add the stock at intervals until the rice is cooked *al-dente* (approximately 25 minutes).
- Add the spinach leaves and half the parmesan, then stir until the spinach has wilted.
- Season to taste, add a little more stock or water if required and serve with the rest of the parmesan and a green leaf salad.

Butternut Squash, Parmesan & Chilli Risotto

Serves 3–4
Cooking time: 35–40 minutes

300g frozen butternut squash, diced
1 teaspoon chilli puree
1 teaspoon garlic puree
300g risotto rice
1 large onion, diced
1 x 600g carton NCG Spicy Butternut Squash & Sweet Potato Soup
100g grated parmesan
50g butter
250ml white wine
300ml vegetable stock (from concentrate or cube)

- Melt the butter in a saucepan and fry the onions until soft. Stir in the butternut squash, chilli and garlic purees and cook for 5 minutes.
- Add the rice and wine, then cook and stir until most of the wine is absorbed. Add the soup and bring to a gentle simmer, stirring frequently.
- Add the stock at intervals until the rice is cooked *al-dente* (approximately 25 minutes).
- Add half the parmesan, season to taste, add a little more stock or water if required, then serve with the rest of the parmesan.

Thai Chicken Noodles

Serves 2–3
Cooking time: 10 minutes

1 x 600g carton NCG Thai Chicken
Fusion Soup
2 x 200g ready-to-wok Thai ribbon
noodles
2 spring onions, cut into long strips
400g Thai-style vegetable stir fry
pack
10g fresh coriander, roughly chopped
2 tablespoons stir fry oil
few shakes lime juice from bottle
(optional)
2 tablespoons roasted peanuts
(optional)

- Heat the oil in a wok, then quickly cook the stir fry vegetables for 2–3 minutes.
- Add the cooked noodles and toss together for a minute or so.
- Add the soup and lime juice before stirring thoroughly.
- Ensure everything is heated through, then serve in deep bowls, topped with the spring onions, coriander and peanuts.

Thai Chicken Curry

Serves 2
Cooking time: 10 minutes

1 x 600g carton NCG Thai Chicken
Fusion Soup
200g cooked chicken breast, sliced
1 tablespoon green Thai curry paste
150g pack baby corn and mangetout

- Cut the baby corn in half lengthways, then heat gently in a saucepan with the soup.
- Once the soup comes to a gentle simmer, cook for 3 minutes.
- Add the mangetout, curry paste and chicken and continue to cook for a further 3–5 minutes until the vegetables are cooked but still crunchy and the chicken is thoroughly heated through.

Serve with a pack of ready-cooked Thai sticky rice, basmati rice or Thai jasmine rice and a scattering of fresh coriander.

Chicken & Vegetable Pie

Serves 4
Cooking time: 35 minutes

1 x 600g carton NCG Chicken Soup
1 teaspoon dried sage
450g prepared stew pack of
vegetables, fresh or frozen (carrots,
onions, swede, turnip, celery)
2 tablespoons garlic oil
400g mini chicken fillets, cubed
375g ready-rolled puff pastry sheets
1 egg, whisked

- Preheat the oven to 200°C/400°F/ gas mark 6.
- Heat the oil in a saucepan, then fry the chicken for 5 minutes.
- Add the vegetables and sage, then cook for a further 5 minutes.
- Add the soup, stir, then bring back to the boil. Transfer to an ovenproof dish.
- Meanwhile, unwrap the pastry sheets, trim the edges and cut into 4 rectangles. Place on a baking sheet, brush with egg, then place in the oven, along with the pie filling.
- Spoon the pie filling into bowls or onto deep plates and top with the cooked pastry.

Serve with steamed green vegetables and creamy mashed potatoes for bigger appetites.

Mushroom & Chicken Pappardelle

Serves 3–4
Cooking time: 15 minutes

1 x 600g carton NCG Wild Mushroom
soup
2 chicken breasts, sliced
250g chestnut mushrooms, sliced
500g bag fresh pappardelle pasta
1 tablespoon olive oil
2 teaspoons green peppercorns in
brine, drained
6 tablespoons grated parmesan
1 tablespoon fresh parsley, chopped

- Heat the oil in a pan and fry the chicken for 2–3 minutes.
- Add the mushrooms and fry until both the chicken and mushrooms are golden.
- Add the soup, gently bring to a simmer, then add the peppercorns.
- Meanwhile, cook the pasta according to the pack instructions and drain.
- Combine the pasta and sauce, add the parsley and toss together.
- Season to taste, sprinkle with parmesan and serve with mixed salad leaves.

Soup
Essentials

Garnishes   Stocks   Larder Ingredients

Soup Essentials

Garnishes

You can have a lot of fun with garnishes. They add taste, texture and decoration to a soup. Your creativity can come to the fore as you match the garnish to the occasion and the guests. In some of the recipes we have suggested particular garnishes that have been tried and tested for that particular soup or dish. In this chapter you'll find lots of inspiration to help you mix and match your own garnishes to your chosen soups.

Almost anything can be used: crisps and breads, puff pastry creations, oils and cream, chopped bacon or sausage, herbs and chopped vegetables. The shapes, colours and tastes will add extra fun to the meal.

Stocks

Good stocks are a foundation of most soups. They're easy and cheap to make, particularly if you plan ahead. With the carcass from your Sunday lunch or a few bones and off-cuts from the butcher or fishmonger, you're ready to go.

Stocks freeze well so you can make them when you have the time and use them as the occasion demands. If you're pressed for time or don't have a pre-prepared stock to hand, a stock cube will do the job.

Larder Ingredients

Of course, the main ingredients for your healthy soup will be fresh. However, many recipes call for a little something extra from the store cupboard so it pays to be ready with some essentials. We've drawn up a list of the main things that are useful to have in your cupboard so you can make yourself a delicious soup whenever you feel the urge.

Oils

A good grassy olive oil adds great flavour to almost every soup. Simply drizzle over the top.

Flavoured oils are also easily available from most supermarkets. Basil, chilli and lemon oils add a lovely touch to many soups, while truffle oil is perfect for adding depth, richness and earthiness.

Lemon & Lime Juice

Lemon juice is great for enhancing the flavours of lots of soups and can often be used instead of salt. If a spicy soup is too spicy, adding a squeeze of lemon or lime will greatly reduce the heat levels. Lime juice will also always go well with fish or any Asian-inspired flavours.

Nuts & Seeds

Many nuts and seeds taste terrific in their natural form; others benefit from being lightly toasted in a dry frying pan – flaked almonds, pine nuts and sesame seeds work brilliantly toasted. Chopped walnuts, pistachio, cashews and hazelnuts are all lovely strewn over a soup, and they work well with cheese too!

Cheese

There are so many classic soup combinations that involve cheese – Broccoli & Stilton, Cauliflower & Cheddar, French Onion & Gruyere. The Italians believe that freshly grated Parmesan is great with almost any soup – the classic being Minestrone – but try it with any vegetable in the squash family.

Save left-over Parmesan rinds and add to a lentil or vegetable soup while cooking – just remember to fish it out before serving.

Grated cheese or cubes are lovely dropped into your bowl and given a quick stir before serving.

A great way to use up small bits of cheese following a dinner party is to grill some cheese on a round of toast and float it on top of your soup; you can change the bread and cheese depending on the soup. Try feta or goats' cheese in a summery red pepper, tomato or courgette soup; Gruyere, cheddar and most blue cheeses are delicious with vegetable soups.

Herbs, Leaves & Vegetables

Chopped fresh herbs are a great addition to almost any soup – chives, basil, mint, coriander and parsley are all favourites of ours.

Finely diced fresh chilli adds unexpected interest and is a great way of pepping up a soup that you made for the whole family but want to give a bit more *oomph* to for the adults.

Some of our favourite vegetable garnishes are:

Spring onions cut into long strips or little slices

Diced or finely sliced red onion, rocket leaves or peppery watercress

Asparagus spears with Parma Ham ...

> Season the asparagus spears, drizzle over a little olive oil, then grill until tender and slightly charred. Meanwhile, grill some whole Parma ham slices until crispy and float both on top of the soup.
>
> Alternatively, wrap 2–3 asparagus spears in a slice of Parma ham then grill until the asparagus is tender and the Parma ham crispy.

Vegetable Crisps

Try either parsnip or beetroot crisps ...

Simply peel and slice very thinly into rounds, then pat dry. Heat some groundnut or vegetable oil in a saucepan (approximately 2cm deep) until smoking, then fry the vegetable slices in small batches for 2–3 minutes each until golden. Drain on kitchen paper, allow to cool, then serve in piles in the middle of the soup.

Pesto

Home-made pesto, like walnut and sage or sundried tomato, as well as fresh ready-prepared pesto, is great for adding interest to your soups. Add a little oil to get a more liquid consistency, then drizzle over the top of the soup.

Fried Delights

Where do we start ...

Meat – fried pancetta cubes; grilled Parma ham; slices of spicy chorizo; strips of chicken; ham off the bone; smoked chicken.

Onions – finely sliced or diced red onions, fried until crisp; little rounds of crispy shallots.

Fish – smoked salmon cut into fine strips; flakes of hot smoked salmon; white crab meat; king prawns in garlic and chilli.

Bread

Bread must be the all-time classic accompaniment to any soup.

A crusty roll; a chunk of granary; sour dough; crusty French stick; bagels; toast; soldiers; croutons; bruschetta; crostini – the list is endless.

Cheese scones fresh from the oven or a savoury muffin would make a welcome addition too.

Croutons

Shop-bought or home-made croutons complement any soup. Here's how we like to make them ...

Don't be tempted to use a frying pan as they will burn very easily.

Preheat your oven to 180°C/350°F/gas mark 4. Take 3 slices of thick sliced, white farmhouse bread and remove the crusts. Cut into approximately 15mm cubes and place in a bowl. Drizzle over 2 tablespoons of olive oil, then toss until coated well. Spread out on a baking tray and bake for 10 minutes until golden.

For garlic croutons, simply use garlic oil; for salt and pepper croutons, just add ground salt and pepper to your oil; for parmesan croutons, add a generous tablespoon of finely grated parmesan to the oil.

Toasts

To make goats' cheese or Gruyere toasts to float on top of your french onion soup, well any soup really ...

Cut a French stick into slices, and make sure the slices fit into your soup bowls. Lightly toast on both sides and top with grated Gruyere or crumbles of goats' cheese. Then either grill the toasts and place on top of your soup or place on top of your soup and grill both the soup and toast together.

Toasties

Children love these – toasted sandwiches cut into strips for dunking or into cubes for floating. Try cheese and onion, cheese and mustard, cheese and ham or blue cheese.

Tortilla Chips

Heat a griddle pan until hot, then take some soft flour tortillas and cook for 2–3 minutes on each side. Cut into wedges and serve.

Pangrattato
Italian-style breadcrumbs

Delicious fried breadcrumbs that can be flavoured with lemon, chilli, thyme or garlic to name but a few! Take 60g of fresh breadcrumbs, 1 clove crushed garlic, 1 teaspoon chopped thyme, 2 tablespoons olive oil, and salt and pepper. Mix together well, then toss into a hot frying pan, stirring continuously until golden.

Crostini

Slice ciabatta or sour dough into 1cm-thick slices and toast on both sides. Rub with the cut side of a garlic clove, drizzle with peppery olive oil and serve.

Try topping with pesto, rouile, aioli, olive tapenade, grated parmesan or goats' cheese.

Cut into different shapes, like hearts or stars, using cookie cutters or a knife. Cookie cutters are great fun for the children; they can make letters, Christmas shapes, teddy bears – the list is endless.

Puff Pastry

Why not make your own cheese straws. They're delicious to dunk.

Use cookie cutters or a knife to make little fish for chowders, or small squares for a mini pie-like topping.

Creamy

A swirl of cream, buttermilk or yogurt, or a dollop of mascarpone cheese, creamy goats' cheese or crème fraîche all add a rich creaminess or cooling element to most soups.

Try mixing freshly chopped herbs, horseradish, sundried tomato paste or cheese in a blender with some cream for a retro-flavoured cream swirl.

Flavoured Butters

Flavoured butters look impressive, taste impressive and can be made in advance – ideal for dinner parties.

They taste great stirred into soups, spread onto warm bread, or melted over potatoes, rice, couscous or pasta.

Simply bring 50g butter (enough to serve 4 people) to room temperature, then mash your desired flavour into it.

The following are all simple but delicious examples, and can be used on their own or in combination: 2 tablespoons snipped chives; 1 clove crushed garlic; 2 tablespoons basil; 2 tablespoons lemon juice with a little zest.

Wrap the flavoured butter in cling film, roll into a small log shape, then chill or freeze until required.

Beef Stock

Makes 8-10 pints

Cooking time: 8 hours

1kg beef bones, chopped into small pieces
500g veal bones (you can substitute the veal bones for beef bones – simply add the quantities together)
6 litres water
2 tablespoons olive oil
3 small carrots, roughly chopped
1 medium onion, roughly chopped
1 large leek, roughly chopped
3 sticks celery, roughly chopped
150g tomatoes, roughly chopped
8 peppercorns, crushed
70g mushrooms, quartered

- Preheat the oven to 200°C/400°F/gas mark 6.
- Remove any excess fat from the bones and place them in a roasting tin. Cook in the oven for 50 minutes.
- Drain off any fat and transfer the bones to a large saucepan.
- Cover with water, bring to the boil and simmer for 20 minutes, skimming well to remove any excess fat.
- Heat the olive oil in another saucepan, then add the carrots, onion, leek and celery. Cook for 10 minutes until browned, but not burnt; add to the pan containing the bones and water.
- Add the tomatoes and peppercorns to the bones and vegetables, bring to the boil and simmer for 6 hours, skimming frequently.
- Sieve the stock into a clean container and seal until required.
- Discard the vegetables and bones.

Chicken Stock

Makes 8–10 pints *Cooking time: 8 hours, 30 minutes*

2kg chicken bones, chopped into small pieces
6 litres water
3 small carrots, roughly chopped
1 medium onion, roughly chopped
1 large leek, roughly chopped
3 sticks celery, roughly chopped
8 peppercorns, crushed

- Place the bones in a large saucepan, add the water, then bring to the boil.
- Simmer for 20 minutes, skimming of any excess fat.
- Add the vegetables and peppercorns and bring back to the boil.
- Simmer for 8 hours, skimming any excess fat frequently.
- Sieve the stock into a clean container and seal until required.
- Discard the vegetables and bones.

Vegetable Stock

Makes 8 pints

Cooking time: 3 hours

4 small carrots, roughly chopped
3 sticks celery, roughly chopped
2 medium leeks, roughly chopped
6 litres water
2 teaspoons peppercorns
1 bay leaf
2 cloves garlic, roughly chopped

- Place the vegetables in a large saucepan, cover with the water and bring to the boil. Simmer for 30 minutes.
- Add the peppercorns, bay leaf and garlic cloves, then bring back to the boil.
- Simmer for 2½ hours, skimming frequently.
- Sieve the stock into a clean container and seal until required.
- Discard the vegetables.

Fish Stock

Makes 10–12 pints　　　Cooking time: 45 minutes

2kg fish bones (sole, turbot or whiting), washed
75g butter
2 medium onions, roughly chopped
6 peppercorns, crushed
25g parsley stalks, roughly chopped
1 lemon, juice of
5 litres water
1 bay leaf

- Melt the butter in a large saucepan, add the onions, peppercorns, parsley stalks and lemon juice, then cook for 15 minutes without browning.
- Add the fish bones and cover and simmer for a further 5 minutes; try to avoid browning.
- Add the bay leaf and water, then bring to the boil and simmer for 20 minutes.
- Remove from the heat and skim off any excess fat.
- Sieve the stock into a clean container and seal until required.
- Discard the vegetables and bones.

Ham Stock

Makes 10–12 pints

Cooking time: 3 hours plus overnight soaking time

1 medium ham hock or joint (900g)
5 litres water
1 onion, roughly chopped
2 carrots, roughly chopped
1 bay leaf
2 celery sticks, roughly chopped
12 peppercorns

- Place the ham in a large saucepan, cover with cold water and soak overnight to remove any excess salt.
- Discard the soaking water. Pour 5 litres of water into the pan and bring to the boil, skimming off any excess fat.
- Add the vegetables, peppercorns and bay leaf, then simmer gently for 2½ to 3 hours until the ham is cooked through.
- Sieve the stock into a clean container and seal until required.
- Discard the ham and vegetables.

Larder Ingredients

As you become even more of a soup enthusiast, you'll want a store cupboard that gives you the freedom to rise to the occasion.

Most of these will keep well, so you can build up a stock as you go, using a little at a time. If you make sure you always have most of these ingredients to hand, you'll only ever have to buy a few fresh ingredients and you'll be able to make any of our delicious soups at the drop of a hat.

When you're using our 'cheats', you may need some frozen ingredients, so there's a list of items for the freezer too.

In the Store Cupboard

Oils
Olive Oil
Truffle Oil
Garlic Oil
Chilli Oil
Basil Oil
Stir Fry Oil

Vinegars
White Wine Vinegar
Red Wine Vinegar
Balsamic Vinegar

Pasta
Macaroni
Linguini
Spaghetti
Mini Pasta for Soup
Lasagne Sheets

Rice & Lentils
Risotto Rice
Paella Rice
Pearl Barley
Red Lentils
Green Lentils
Puy Lentils

Vegetables & Beans
Tinned Chopped Tomatoes
Tomato Puree
Passata
Tinned Artichoke Hearts
Tinned Cannellini Beans
Tinned Red Kidney Beans
Tinned Chick Peas
Flame Roasted Red Peppers

Herbs & Spices
Ground Cinnamon
Ground Cumin
Turmeric
Garam Masala
Chilli Flakes
Chilli Powder
Sweet Smoked Paprika
Whole Nutmeg
Bay Leaves
Saffron
Sea Salt
Peppercorns
Green Peppercorns in brine
Sage
Oregano

Sauces, Pastes & Jellies

Worcestershire Sauce
Horseradish Sauce
Soy Sauce
Fish Sauce
Redcurrant Jelly
Green Thai Curry Paste

Mustards

Wholegrain
Dijon

On occasions when we need to cheat...

Passata with onions & garlic
Tinned Chopped Tomatoes with garlic & herbs
Stock – Concentrated Liquid/Bouillon/Cubes
Fresh breadcrumbs
Tinned Red Kidney Beans in Chilli Sauce
Tinned Mixed Beans
Tinned Ready-Fried Onions
Ready-Cooked Noodles
Miso Soup Sachets

Coconut Milk
Coconut Cream
Dried Porcini Mushrooms
Honey
Dried Apricots
Dried Prunes
Caster Sugar
Icing Sugar
Plain Flour
Chocolate (70% Cocoa)

In the Fridge

Dairy

Milk

Double Cream

Single Cream

Soured Cream

Crème Fraîche

Natural Yogurt

Butter

Eggs

On occasions when we need to cheat ...

Shortcrust Pastry Case

Ready-Rolled Puff Pastry Sheets

Ready-Cooked Chicken

Fresh Cheese Sauce

Bottled Lime Juice

Bottled Lemon Juice

Fresh Pesto

Grated Parmesan

Fresh Gnocchi

Chilli Puree

Ginger Puree

Garlic Puree

Lemongrass Puree

In the Freezer for when we need to cheat

Prepared Frozen Vegetables

Butternut Squash, Diced

Sweet Potato, Diced

Onions, Diced

Soya Beans

Mashed Potato

Grilled Vegetables

Broad Beans

Stew Pack Vegetable Mix

Sliced Mushrooms

Index

Tomatoes continued

U, V

W

X, Y, Z

Notes

Notes

Notes

Notes

Notes

Notes

Notes

Notes